The Power of Innovative Thinking

Getting Outside the Box

Written by Jim Wheeler
Edited by National Press Publications

NATIONAL PRESS PUBLICATIONS
A Division of Rockhurst College Continuing Education Center, Inc.
6901 West 63rd Street • P.O. Box 2949 • Shawnee Mission, Kansas 66201-1349
1-800-258-7248 • 1-913-432-7757

National Seminars endorses nonsexist language. In an effort to make this handbook clear, consistent and easy to read, we've used "he" throughout the odd-numbered chapters and "she" throughout the even-numbered chapters. The copy is not intended to be sexist.

The Power of Innovative Thinking — *Getting Outside the Box*
Published by National Press Publications, Inc.
Copyright 1995, National Press Publications, Inc.
A Division of Rockhurst College Continuing Education Center, Inc.

Printed in the United States of America

12 13 14 15

ISBN 1-55852-139-9

Table of Contents

FOREWORD

The Power of Innovative Thinking will give you an advantage over your competitors. While they're busy working harder, you'll be able to work smarter! Rather than attacking problems with muscle and might, you'll learn to "think" your way to success.

The tools and techniques discussed in *The Power of Innovative Thinking* are ones that I have used in business, education and my personal life. While I have my favorites, I always rethink new situations and try other tools until I find one that works for me. You can do the same. Find tools that work for you — and have fun along the way!

I hope you enjoy "tickling" your mind on your way to discovering what success is all about.

— J. Wheeler

1 THINKING ABOUT THINKING

"The significant problems we face cannot be solved at the same level of thinking we were at when we created them."
— *Albert Einstein*

What Is Thinking?

In today's fast-paced, continually changing business world, you need powerful thinking skills to make decisions quickly and — more importantly — effectively. To be successful, you must know why you think the way you do and how to use your natural thinking abilities to your best advantage.

If you keep thinking in the same old way, you'll arrive at the same old conclusions and leave behind a well-worn rut of business-as-usual decisions. Trains must go where the tracks lead; they cannot follow unplanned routes. Similarly, if we always think along the same tracks, we'll probably arrive at the same destination. But if we use a helicopter for our journey, we're not limited by "tracks."

The Power of Innovative Thinking will assist you in making better decisions by helping you to better understand your thinking abilities. In addition, it will give you the tools to effectively solve problems. Specifically, after reading this insightful and motivational book, you'll be able to:

1. Reduce negative thinking barriers

2. Avoid one-dimensional thinking

3. View old problems in a new light

4. Uncover the opportunities in every problem

5. Think more quickly and accurately

6. Avoid falling into common thinking traps

7. Move successfully from idea to action to success

8. Find new answers

9. Discover your own thinking style

10. Make better decisions

Thinking is the conscious use of our minds to reason, deliberate, debate, predict and reflect on a subject. By better understanding why humans think the way they do, you'll learn how to approach problems in ways that lead to better decision-making. By smoothing out the ruts that have formed in the past, you'll be better equipped to "rethink" your responses when faced with new problems and opportunities. You don't need to be a victim of doing what has always been done.

Emotions vs. Thinking

Our brain gives us sets of two messages — one for thinking and another for emotions. Our eyes, ears, nose, taste buds and sense of feel produce sensations of pain and pleasure that tend to rule our actions.

For example, you may have planned to spend the evening with your family discussing next year's vacation. As you arrive home, your neighbor asks you to play tennis after dinner. Logically, you know the vacation plans are important to your family; however, you receive a lot of pleasure — a sensory reaction — from playing tennis with your neighbor. A conflict results between your logic and your emotions.

Or perhaps your manager has given you the job of streamlining the production line to increase productivity. After a lot of work and thought, you know that the best alternative is to install new equipment that will result in laying off three people. The people who will lose their jobs are your friends. The logic part of your brain tells you the correct action. Emotionally, you want to avoid hurting your friends.

Through the years, you have learned to conform to both written and unwritten rules that lead to success in your personal life. If you want to be successful in your business decisions, you must resolve the conflict between emotion and logic.

Resolving Mental Conflict

By resolving the conflict between logical thinking and emotion, we gain new insights into how to think in different ways. Most of what we have learned has come from people of influence such as parents, teachers, peers and friends. That learning has produced filters that may distort the information we receive. For example, when we were children, we were taught that people should keep their promises. Our value filters want us to believe that people in the business world will keep their promises. Logical thinking — and good practice — warns us, "Get it in writing!"

Or perhaps you grew up next door to immigrants from the country of Boldavia (not a real country). They were rowdy and lived like slobs. As a result, when you meet a Boldavian at work, your filters automatically pin a label on that person — a rowdy slob!

While we must be alert and sensitive to the potential negative effects of filters, filters can be beneficial! They allow us to sort information and discard what is not important. Imagine what would happen if you had to remember all the information with which you're confronted each day.

Weather forecasts, news, family plans, sounds you hear on the car radio while driving to work, your appointment schedule, your associates' appointment schedules and information about your company's new products as well as the competitor's new products, all draw your attention. Confronted with such an onslaught of information, filters help you highlight which items are important. The three types of filters that influence your thinking are:

- Subconscious filters

  — Values

  — Culture and heritage

  — Religion

- Survival filters

- Social filters

Subconscious Filters

Subconscious filters automatically open the door to our values, culture and heritage, and religious background. We do the "right thing" because our unconscious filters tell us to do the "right thing."

For example, if you are a thrifty individual, you may be cautious about waste and how your organization's resources are used. While this value may be an asset to a loan officer, it could be a liability when it's time to decide how much money to spend on research and development.

Or just suppose you feel that people with green noses are lazy and unreliable, and therefore you are reluctant to hire people with green noses. However, your personal value system may be in conflict with employment policies regarding discrimination issues. This conflict has never been more important than now, since the Equal Employment Opportunity Act and the Americans with Disabilities Act affect personnel decisions.

Some cultures recognize special holidays. For example, salespersons from the East Coast might find customers unavailable if they plan sales calls for May 5 (Cinco de Mayo) in the Southwest. Those unfamiliar with

Patriot's Day, a state holiday in Massachusetts, would encounter similar frustration.

Perhaps your religious upbringing has taught you that Sunday is a day of rest. Therefore, your business remains closed on Sunday. Customers who normally work Monday through Friday may be looking for your product on the weekend. If your competitors are open on Sunday, you lose potential revenue. If your religious beliefs are stronger than your desire to increase profits, you will remain closed on Sunday. Your unconscious filter controlled your business decision.

"Trigger" Words

When we hear certain words or phrases, messages from our subconscious filters can "trigger" emotions. It may be the name of someone we dislike very much, or words that recall pleasant experiences. "New and improved," "audit," "customer service" or "overtime" are typical examples of words that trigger certain emotions. When we are aware of these trigger words, we can control the filter, monitor our feelings and rethink the issue.

Becoming Aware of Subconscious Filters

You can become aware of and subsequently take control of your subconscious filters by answering the following questions. Ask someone you trust to review your answers to these questions with you to benefit from his insight.

1. Values

   • What values do I subscribe to with a passion?

   • What does my company value?

   • How might these values complement one other?

   • How might these values conflict?

   • How can I resolve conflicts between my personal values and my organization's values?

2. Cultural/heritage

- What behaviors are associated with my heritage and culture?

- What behaviors do my associates, customers, and clients display that, in my mind, indicate their heritage and culture?

- How can I resolve differences between my own and others' culture and heritage that affect my thinking?

- What positive and negative reactions does my culture and heritage prompt from others?

3. Religious background

- What are my religious beliefs?

- How do these beliefs help or hinder me in my business relationships?

- What positive and negative reactions do my religious beliefs prompt in others?

4. "Trigger" words

- What are some "trigger" words that stir up my emotions and interfere with my thinking abilities?

- What specific emotions are affected by these "trigger" words?

Survival Filters

Human beings have built-in survival filters to prevent sensory overload. Sound filters, for example, usually prevent us from hearing sounds that aren't important to us. To become aware of how this works, sit quietly in a comfortable place, close your eyes and listen. Do you hear the motor in your computer? The hum of a laser printer or copy machine? The phone ringing in a distant office? When you are focused and concentrating on your work, you usually don't hear these sounds. However, sudden noises of a different frequency — your telephone ringing or a colleague calling your name — almost always grab your attention.

We also have memory filters that serve as our "auto-pilot." They let us perform routine tasks while we're consciously thinking of something else. For example, memory filters allow us to drive home while we're thinking about what to have for dinner. Learning a new task such as typing or operating machinery requires much thought and concentration. But once we are skilled at the task, we no longer need to think through the steps — they become automatic.

Memory filters are time-savers that can cause us to make mistakes and miss opportunities. For example, Brent, a well-respected electrician in a factory, could fix anything — find the problem and Brent could fix it. The power cord on a machine that moved back and forth needed to be fixed at least twice a week. Brent could see that the insulation around the cord was always broken in a different place. Without much thought, he would work his magic on the cord, and the machine could be used again. Fixing the cord had become a habit with Brent. Rather than thinking through the problem, he just fixed the cord — his memory filter was working. One evening, the shop supervisor was working overtime and saw the real problem that Brent had failed to see — the insulation on the power cord was a treat for a family of mice. When we are solving problems and making decisions, we need to check our memory filters once in a while to be sure that we are defining the real problem.

Using Survival Filters to Your Advantage

Survival filters can be an asset to your career if you know which tasks should be routine and which tasks require more concentration. List the tasks that you perform frequently. Consider the following questions so you can improve the way you use your survival filters.

1. What tasks do I routinely perform without much thought?

2. On which of these tasks should I focus more attention? Why?

3. What tasks should I learn to perform in a routine manner?

7

4. What steps will I take to recognize when a task requires more concentration? Consider the following:

- Have I always solved problems in the same way?

- Are my results always the same?

- Do others come up with better results?

For example, answering the telephone whenever it rings has become a habit for many of us. We may answer it even when someone is in our office talking to us. You can improve your communication skills by examining this sound filter. Do you need to answer the telephone just because it is ringing? How do you think this makes your visitor feel? Can you ask someone else to answer the phone or use voice-mail if it's available?

Social Filters

Our social filters determine how we behave at work, at home and in our careers. They contain written and unwritten rules that dictate how we act in different situations. In short, social filters tell us what we "should" do.

For instance, when we meet people socially, we usually call them by their first name. In a business setting, however, we usually use the title of respect and the person's last name until we are given permission to do otherwise. Consider:

- Do you answer the telephone the same way at home as you do in the office?

- Do you greet visitors at work in the same manner you welcome guests to your home?

- Do you prepare your office budget the same way you prepare your personal budget?

Thinking about Social Filters

To help recognize your social filters, answer the following questions.

1. How might your behavior differ when meeting an unfamiliar child selling candy at your front door as opposed to meeting the child of an associate at work selling the same candy?

2. How would you respond to an offer to attend a major sporting event with your supervisor vs. the same offer from your brother-in-law?

3. How might your response differ when someone requests a charitable contribution at your home vs. the same request from a business associate?

4. How would you behave differently when your significant other asks you to lunch vs. a business associate of the opposite gender?

When you can recognize appropriate behavior and use your thinking skills in similar situations, you will be in control of your social filters.

When you have a better understanding of your subconscious, survival and social filters, you can take control of your thinking skills. And when you are in control of your thinking skills, you'll make more effective decisions!

Framing

When your subconscious, survival and social filters interact with your desires, goals and aspirations, you have a frame of reference. Your frame of reference — or framing — influences the decisions you make and how you respond to challenges. Figure 1-1 shows how this might look on your wall if you think of "framing" as a picture frame.

FRAMING

Figure 1-1.

Understanding your frame of reference gives you greater control over your end results, because you will be able to separate your logical thinking from your emotions. Understanding frames also gives you insight into how other people think and act.

Anchoring

While framing provides a "picture frame" that tends to define boundaries, anchors form a point of reference. Both framing and anchoring can restrict your thinking.

For example, by adding only one line, change the following picture so that it has a value of 6.

Most people see the Roman numerals I and X. Because they are made of straight lines, people tend to "anchor" themselves on the concept of straight lines, then look for another straight line to solve the problem. Another straight line is not the solution. A line can also be curved. The answer to this problem, then, is to place a curved line in front of the "IX" to form the word "SIX."

SIX

But anchoring can also help us. For example, let's say your manager tells you to send a memo to the employees in your department to find out who's available to work overtime. The key words "memo," "employees," "department," "available" and "overtime" provide anchors, or points of reference. Because of these anchors, you know exactly what your boss wants you to do.

Imagine the potential confusion and embarrassment if people were not anchored in certain business practices. When you tell an employee to entertain a visiting client while you finish an important telephone call, you expect the word "entertain" will create an anchor, or image, of certain acceptable business behavior. If the employee has a different anchor for the word "entertain" than you do, however, the visiting client may be subjected to a juggling act or a tap dance.

Anchoring Others

To influence others, you need to have a starting point for communicating. For example, when you tell your staff that you are having a meeting to discuss next year's budget, they have an idea of what you will be talking about. However, if you were to tell them you are going to discuss the effect of a decline in the price-earnings ratio of nonconvertible debentures on the availability of operational and capital resources for the succeeding year, they would probably have no idea what will be discussed.

When people start at the anchor, you can communicate with them in one of three zones — the "Safe Zone," the "Aha Zone" and the "Danger Zone."

The Safe Zone

When you communicate information that is understood by both you and the other person, you are operating in the Safe Zone. When anchored in the Safe Zone, people are comfortable and usually respond as anticipated. If a topic is introduced that is not understood by both people, you can remain in the Safe Zone only if you and the other person are aware of each other's limits of knowledge.

Case Study: 1-1.

Roger is a financial wizard who knows all there is to know about finance and accounting. Clare Marie is a computer expert who can make letters and numbers dance across any computer screen. As long as Roger understands Clare Marie's limited knowledge of accounting and Clare Marie is aware of Roger's limited knowledge of computers, the two can safely discuss how to integrate Roger's accounting work into a new software program. When Roger begins speaking of contra accounts and price-earnings ratios, Clare Marie may become uncomfortable. When Clare Marie speaks of bits and gigabytes spinning into the computer's RAM, Roger may become uncomfortable with the new software program.

Each person has neglected to recognize the limitations of the other and has stepped out of the Safe Zone. As a result, communication will suffer, or will stop altogether.

The Aha Zone

When you move from what people realize they know to information they didn't realize they knew, you are in the Aha Zone. The pathway to the Aha Zone is blazed by making new associations built upon current information.

Case Study: 1-2.

Diane is an excellent administrator with a knack for getting the most out of people. Consequently, she was asked to lead the committee formed to write the company's mission statement. Diane knew she could influence people to work cooperatively, but she was worried that she didn't have the writing skills necessary to compose a clear statement. As the mission statement began to take shape, however, Diane realized that she knew more about writing than she'd thought. This inner excitement motivated her to successfully lead her committee.

The Danger Zone

The Danger Zone, as the name implies, is a dangerous place to anchor when you communicate. When you anchor in the Danger Zone, you'll hear phrases like, "Those people are out of their environment," and ". . . like a fish out of water."

Case Study: 1-3.

Danny, the company's top salesman, was appointed by the CEO to the position of Human Resources Director because of his excellent ability to get along with people. Danny knew there was much to learn, but he failed to realize just how much legal information was involved with the job. Because of his lack of legal knowledge, he made hasty decisions that resulted in confusion and distrust among associates. Conversation about Danny usually started with, "He's a nice guy, but . . . ."

The content of the message you send to others will determine the location of the anchor. By changing the message content, you can make people feel comfortable, instill excitement, or you can cause them to mistrust you and even stop communicating.

ANCHORING ZONE	AWARENESS LEVEL	CONTENT OF MESSAGE
AHA	*Unaware of how much you know*	Known Information
SAFE	*Aware of how much you know and don't know*	Unknown Information
DANGER	*Unaware of how much you don't know*	

Figure 1-2.

Anchoring for Successful Results

When you make good use of your thinking skills, you'll know ahead of time where you want to anchor yourself and others. In Case Study No. 1-1, Roger and Clare Marie will respect one another's abilities as long as they remain in the Safe Zone. Diane, in Case Study No. 1-2, has the potential to lead successful future projects because she gained confidence while working in the Aha Zone. In Case Study No. 1-3, the CEO placed Danny in the Danger Zone and the company was forced to suffer the consequences.

Deciding where to anchor yourself and your associates requires careful consideration of everyone's abilities. For example, when you need to make decisions, you'll be most successful if you start in the Safe Zone. Moving toward the Aha Zone may produce successful results as it rewards people for their efforts and initiative. In the Danger Zone, strong leadership skills will be necessary to guide people around anchoring points. You need to know what information may be requested by others and make it readily available. Ask yourself what the people involved will need to know that they don't know now.

The following guide will help you decide where you want to anchor your communication. The zone that you choose depends on how much you know about a topic.

I . . .	THE APPROPRIATE ZONE
. . . am aware of what I know.	SAFE
. . . am aware of what I don't know.	
. . . am aware of what I know.	AHA
. . . am not aware of what I know.	
. . . am aware of what I don't know.	DANGER
. . . am not aware of what I don't know.	

Figure 1-3.

Paradigms

Paradigms (pronounced **pare**-uh-dimes) are a combination of frames and anchors that establish and define your decisions and actions at work. A paradigm is a generally accepted system that makes rules for acceptable behavior, attitudes, and actions that are necessary for success. For example, the "proper business attire" in most corporate offices is a suit for men and a dress or suit for women. There may be no written rules that state this policy — it's just understood. This paradigm, called "the business world," has created its own rules.

In another example, when the Chrysler Corporation was in financial trouble, Lee Iacocca cut his own salary to $1. The paradigm included belt-tightening for all employees. Iacocca wanted the respect of his employees, so he changed his anchor, or point of reference. He was no longer working for money, but for the welfare of the company.

Thomas Watson, the founder of IBM, once stated that there was only room for about five kinds of computers in the entire world. Consistent with this view, for many years, IBM focused on producing large computers. After losing most of the personal computer market to competitors, IBM made a paradigm shift, meaning that IBM changed its set of references. The corporation had to rethink its position, meet the needs of buyers, and become a manufacturer of PCs.

Anchors are located in frames, frames are located in paradigms, and our actions within a paradigm can be controlled by anchors within the paradigm. For example, in the business world (the paradigm), we may be encouraged to care for the needy (the frame) by giving to the employer's favorite charity (the anchor).

In some cases, there will be a shift, or change, in the paradigm that will force the anchor to change. For example:

- *The Paradigm:* "I've been working for The Company for 10 years. My father worked here for 40 years. The Company takes care of us."

- *The Frame:* "Because I'm a hard worker and loyal to The Company, I'll be taken care of."

15

- ***The Anchor:*** "We all succeed at The Company — there'll always be a job."

- ***The Paradigm Shift:*** "Money Buckets, Inc. lost money for the first time in its history. There will be no pay raises."

In some cases, we change our paradigm, and that affects our anchor. For instance:

- ***The Paradigm:*** "I have worked for Old Standby for 15 years. Old Standby pays well and has good benefits."

- ***The Frame:*** "Because Old Standby has good benefits, I get free medical insurance."

- ***The Anchor:*** "I never have to worry about sickness or injury costs because my medical insurance will take care of the bills."

- ***The Paradigm Change:*** "I decided to take a job with My Dream Company because I've always wanted to work there, and they offered me a 15 percent salary increase. My Dream Company doesn't have medical insurance for its employees."

To be a successful decision-maker, you need to keep your eye on the paradigm and be ready for changes that may affect your anchor. Successful thinking and decision-making within a paradigm depend on your mental flexibility.

The Thinking Box

Throughout ***The Power of Innovative Thinking***, you'll meet The Thinking Box. It gives you a chance to immediately personalize what you have just read. By completing the exercise in The Thinking Box, you will remember the information more easily, and you'll be more successful using the tools and techniques you've just learned in the real world.

Personal Life	**Career**
Identify the paradigms, frames, and anchors that affect your personal life.	*Identify the paradigms, frames, and anchors that affect your career or your workplace.*
The Thinking Box	
Identify the paradigms, frames, and anchors that affect how you solve problems.	*Identify the paradigms, frames, and anchors that affect your personal and career growth.*
Problem-Solving	**Growth**

Summary

In this chapter you learned about:

- The conflict between emotions and thinking

- Subconscious, social, and survival filters

- How filters create frames and anchors

- The Safe, Aha and Danger anchoring zones

- Frames and anchors within paradigms

When you understand frames, anchors and paradigms, you can better understand your thinking style and learn how to make more effective decisions.

In the next chapter of *The Power of Innovative Thinking*, you'll identify your primary thinking style. You'll also learn pitfalls to avoid when you "rethink" your way to effective decisions.

2 THINKING STYLES

*"Judgment and imagination can help each other
if kept apart when they should be kept apart."*
— Alex F. Osborn

When forced to make a decision, people take different mental routes to arrive at that decision. Like travelers you may know, some take the most direct route to get where they're going. Others think of all the routes available, select the best one and then go. Still others take the scenic tour and enjoy the journey. And some people jump in the car and just go, giving little thought to direction or destination.

Identifying Your Thinking Style

To better understand the mental route you take when solving problems and making decisions, you need to know your thinking style. Once you understand your thinking style, you'll be able to select the best thinking tools, techniques and strategies to use in different situations. The following informal survey will shed some light on your thinking style. Choose either *a* or *b*.

1. When a new computer software program is loaded on your computer, you prefer to

   a) proceed through the tutorial

   b) start using the program right away, learning through trial and error

2. You prefer to

   a) vary your route to and from work

   b) always take the same route to and from work

3. When dining out, you usually

   a) order the same foods

   b) order different foods most every time

4. When taking notes during meetings or conferences, your notes are

   a) usually covered with doodles

   b) neat and well organized

5. When you travel by car to a distant city, you prefer to

   a) plan your route and stick to it

   b) plan a number of routes and decide which way to go once you're on the road

6. When faced with a number of different tasks at work, you prefer to

   a) work on several tasks at one time

   b) complete one task before starting on the next

7. When required to learn new and difficult material, you prefer to

   a) study one source of information

   b) use different sources of information

8. Your desk at work or home contains

   a) a wide variety of pens and pencils

   b) one or only a few writing tools

9. The files in your desk are

   a) arranged in a logical manner that most people would understand

   b) arranged in such a way that only you can find anything

10. You prefer to associate with people who

    a) have many different and varied interests

    b) have interests similar to yours

Add together the *a's* selected for the odd-numbered questions and the *b's* selected for the even-numbered questions. These choices represent an adaptive style of thinking. If you have eight or more, you tend to use an adaptive thinking style. If your total is three or less, you tend to use an innovative style of thinking. If your score is between three and eight, the situation usually dictates which thinking style you use. Neither the adaptive nor the innovative style of thinking is "right" or "wrong."

The Adaptive Thinking Style

Adaptive thinkers tend to:

- Follow established patterns

- Be well organized

- Focus on the goal

- Be pleased when the decision is made

- Be comfortable handling one task at a time

- Prefer to learn through one source

Adaptive thinkers are usually at their best within a well-defined paradigm, meaning that they follow the rules of the established system. Adaptive thinkers are usually satisfied only when a goal is reached, and they prefer to complete one task before moving on to another. They may get locked into an anchor that prevents them from making changes fast, but by being locked in they offer stability during periods of change.

The Innovative Thinking Style

A score of three or less on the previous survey indicates that you tend to be an innovative thinker. Innovative thinkers tend to:

- Use different ways to get results

- Appear unorganized

- Value the process more than the actual goal

- Prefer to continue the process rather than reach the goal

- Be involved in more than one activity or task at a time

- Prefer to learn through more than one source

While innovative thinkers usually work within the system, they also go outside to look for answers. They may attempt to change the rules or redefine the system along the way. Innovative thinkers usually appear to be in a constant state of movement and seem unorganized. They often get great pleasure while working through the process and may even be disappointed when the goal is reached. "Many irons in the fire" was probably first used to describe innovative thinkers.

Need for a Balance of Thinking Styles

To be successful in business, you need to be able to effectively use the tools and techniques of both innovative and adaptive thinking. If you are an adaptive thinker, innovative thinking techniques will get you out of the rut of always doing things the same way. If you are an innovative thinker, on the other hand, adaptive thinking techniques will help keep you organized and more goal-oriented. Depending on the situation and desired results, you will find the tools and techniques of each thinking style can be beneficial to you.

For example, when you are looking for new ways to develop a prospect list, innovative thinking tools will be useful as you'll be able to think of more ways to find prospects than by resorting to the tools of the adaptive thinking style. Similarly, when selecting someone for promotion, you will find adaptive thinking tools more useful, because you will focus on the end result rather than on merely finding more people for promotion.

Groups — teams, committees, task forces — can benefit from a mix of people with different thinking styles. An effective leader will choose both innovative thinkers and adaptive thinkers when forming a group. Adaptive thinkers keep innovative thinkers in touch with the reality of the paradigm; innovative thinkers help adaptive thinkers see beyond the individual steps of a plan. Adaptive thinkers keep innovative thinkers goal-oriented and make sure the project is completed. In other words, the two thinking styles complement each other.

Pitfalls to Avoid

When using new tools and techniques to develop your thinking skills, be aware of the following pitfalls:

Time. When pressed for time and in high-stress situations, rely on tried-and-tested tools and techniques to get results fast. Use new tools and techniques when you have time to experiment and possibly need time to correct mistakes that may occur while you learn something new.

"It Always Worked in the Past." Just because a familiar technique or strategy has worked in the past doesn't necessarily mean it will work in the future. One constant in business is change, and change usually occurs when you least expect it. Rules can change. When they do, you can be ready if you have rehearsed new techniques and strategies.

Effect of Results. When learning how to use new tools and techniques, work on problems that have little effect on your workplace. Start with small decisions — file organization, parking assignments, recreational events — before taking on the big ones like company reorganization, changes in personnel policies or changing marketing strategies. This will provide a way for you to perfect and adapt your new-found thinking tools and techniques.

The Paradigm. Know your paradigm! Some paradigms are more willing or capable than others to accept and use new tools and techniques. You may need to prove to others that a new thinking tool is useful on small tasks before tackling major projects. Then you can encourage others to use powerful thinking tools.

Summary

This chapter has made you aware of your dominant thinking style. You learned the characteristics of adaptive thinkers and innovative thinkers and the importance of balancing the two thinking styles. You also discovered some of the pitfalls you may encounter when attempting to use new thinking tools and techniques.

In Chapter 3, you'll learn the differences in problem-solving, opportunity-seeking and decision-making, and how you can best use your thinking style. You will also become familiar with the characteristics of reactive and proactive climates and begin to use the Friends and Frustraters Tool.

3 PROBLEM-SOLVING, OPPORTUNITY-SEEKING AND DECISION-MAKING

"Every activity is a process and can be improved."
— *W. Edwards Deming*

People often go through their daily activities without being aware of the thinking skills it takes to perform those activities. We dress for work, drive our car and use the telephone without giving it much thought. In the previous chapter, you learned about the adaptive and innovative thinking styles that you may have been using unconsciously up till now. Chapter 3 will show you how to use specific thinking skills more deliberately in the workplace when solving problems and making decisions.

The Reactive Climate

The work climate of any company is set by the organization's leaders and the personalities of the people who work there. A *reactive* climate is a work environment that usually waits for something to happen and then responds. In the business world, that "something" is usually caused by forces outside the workplace, such as customers, the community or government. If nothing pushes the reactive climate, the status quo is maintained.

For example, for years the defense industry operated in a reactive climate. As long as there was a need for military equipment, defense-related companies survived and saw no need to figure out what they would do in the future. As a result, when there were major cutbacks in military spending, many companies went bankrupt.

25

In a reactive climate, managers are measured by their ability to be speedy problem solvers. Terms like "fire fighter" and "crisis manager" describe these individuals. They rely on thinking skills oriented toward problem-solving and quick decision-making and are usually crisis-oriented.

The Proactive Climate

With rapid changes in business, the role of the problem-solver has changed. If you want your organization to be successful today, you need to recognize, establish and nurture a *proactive* climate where energy is spent finding ways to prevent problems *before* they happen. In a proactive climate, you must anticipate problems, needs and changes rather than wait for a crisis. Military personnel, for example, often prepare contingency plans before an operation is launched. Computer users back up their hard drive onto floppies in case the hard drive crashes. Many companies have "disaster" plans in the event of a major catastrophe.

People in the proactive climate use phrases like, "If it happens, we know what to do," "No sweat! We've already thought of that possibility," and "If the zazzle flute doesn't fit, then the giggle gear will." They are prepared — "just in case."

When you are aware of your work climate, you'll be able to use the proper thinking skills. Reactive climates require problem-solving tools and techniques. In the proactive climate, you'll need innovative thinking skills that help you come up with more than one option or solution to a problem. Clearly, some tools and techniques work better in a reactive climate than in a proactive climate, and vice versa. Before you select thinking-skills tools and techniques, you first need to determine if your work climate is reactive or proactive. Once you've determined that, you'll be more successful at using your thinking-skills tools and techniques. *The key concept is to determine the type of climate you're in before you select your strategies, techniques and tools.*

Strategies, Techniques, and Tools

What's the difference among strategies, techniques, and tools? Consider the following:

Strategies are similar to blueprints used to build a house. They provide a broad picture of how everyone will get to the anticipated goal, which is the finished house. Strategies are the long-range plans and are hard to change. In business, Total Quality Management and reengineering may mean drawing up a whole new plan, and making these plans work requires powerful thinking skills.

Techniques are the instructions and procedures that tell you how to operate a particular tool. If the blueprint indicates that the house will be built of wood, it might be safe to assume that the technique will involve joining the wood with nails. Doing things better and faster with fewer resources is the standard operating procedure in many organizations; however, management techniques, job descriptions and pay rates may not match the new strategies. You need to stay on top of new techniques to ensure success in your job.

Tools are the devices used to do the actual work. To drive nails, you'll need a hammer; however, the blueprints may or may not specify whether the hammer is to be the standard hand-held type or a power nailer. Since most plans don't tell us which tool to use, we need to experiment with new, different, and sometimes better tools. That's what continuous self-improvement is all about — learning new tools and techniques so we can survive in the constantly changing business world.

Facing Challenges

When confronted with a challenge, you first need to determine if your work climate is reactive or proactive. In most cases, you probably already know; however, take a moment to assess the situation. Changes may have occurred that will contaminate the issue. The people in your organization may have changed, or the organization itself may have changed. Rather than just assuming that the work climate is the same as it was yesterday, spend a few moments thinking about it.

Then assess the challenge — will you be solving a problem or seeking new opportunities? For example, for the fifth time in a month, a customer has threatened to cancel a substantial order if it's not received within three working days. If you see this situation as a problem, your strategy will probably be to find a way to speed up the delivery of this order, as you have done with the previous four. On the other hand, if you see this situation as an opportunity to improve your delivery service, your strategy may end up resulting in a new delivery system.

In this example, the two strategies used tell us how to deal with the situation. If the strategy is to provide immediate customer satisfaction, then we'll solve the problem with little or no thought about the future. We'll use the same techniques and tools we've used four times before. However, if the strategy is to provide customer satisfaction now and in the future, we'll question how well the tools and techniques we've used before will work this time. We may need to find new ones. When we solve the immediate problem by using a new strategy, we hope to eliminate this type of problem for good.

Problem-Solving

In a reactive climate, the problem-solving process usually starts when a crisis is in progress. A solution is needed — fast! People react to the situation and attempt to fix it. If the same thinking skills are used that have always been used, there's a good chance that the solutions you get will be the same as you always got in the past. When under pressure, people tend to operate in the way they always have. Old strategies rarely produce new results, and outdated techniques and tools may be too slow to keep up with today's business climate.

Opportunity-Seeking

Opportunity-seeking uses the same thinking skills as problem-solving, except time usually isn't a key factor. Instead, opportunity-seeking usually is found in a proactive rather than a reactive climate because people seek opportunities to prevent future problems. An opportunity-seeking climate is the best place to try out new thinking strategies, techniques and tools, since there is usually little or no pressure to find an immediate solution.

Decision-Making

When we face a challenge, we get the best results when we know what thinking skills are needed. As Figure 3-1 illustrates, the thinking skills associated with decision-making are present in every challenge you face, whether in the form of problem-solving or opportunity-seeking.

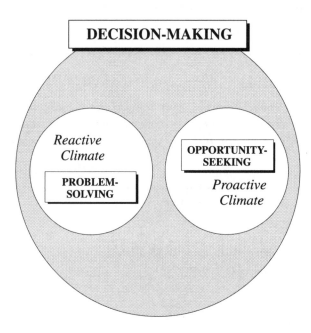

Figure 3-1.

Decisions are usually made on the basis of *Yes, No,* or *No Decision.* That is, when you make a decision, you judge the correctness of the decision based on whether or not it solves a problem. Does it? *Yes? No?* If you don't have enough information, you can decide *No Decision.* For instance, when you buy a new car, you may know what you want. Suppose you want a new car that gets 30 miles to the gallon and has cruise control and air conditioning. As you look at each model, you decide *Yes* or *No.* However, if you are merely looking through a showroom window, you might see a car you like, but you don't have enough information because you can't see what options it has. So you may decide *No Decision.* Problem-solvers and opportunity-seekers can work in both reactive and proactive climates. The thinking skills used depend upon the climate as well as the activity.

Personal Life	**Career**
Identify the paradigms, frames, and anchors that affect your personal life.	*Identify the paradigms, frames, and anchors that affect your career or your workplace.*
The Thinking Box	
Identify the paradigms, frames, and anchors that affect how you solve problems.	*Identify the paradigms, frames, and anchors that affect your personal and career growth.*
Problem-Solving	**Growth**

Framing, Anchoring and Decision-Making

We are often forced into making decisions in our personal lives and careers based on emotions rather than logic. Your child says, "You love me; so you'll let me have the car." Your supervisor says, "You get along well with your associates, so help them out and work next weekend." When emotions are added to the decision-making process, we may react immediately rather than make a conscious effort to think out the situation.

When we examine the logic behind people's requests, however, we find that many requests are illogical, and we are better able to focus on the issue at hand. For example, loving your child is only vaguely related to the car, and getting along well with your co-workers doesn't logically mean "I am the best," or the only choice to work this weekend. *The logic is flawed.* If you recognize you're being anchored by your emotions, you realize that the possession of your car has nothing to do with how much you love your child, and you can then make a rational decision based on facts rather than an emotional anchor.

The same is true of the request to work next weekend. Your supervisor has tried to use your compassion for your associates as an anchor for your decision-making. Rather than basing your decision on that emotional anchor, use your thinking skills to make the decision. Is it appropriate for you to work next weekend or not?

Avoiding the Rut

Some decisions are made out of habit. For example, most of us rarely make a conscious decision to answer the phone when it rings. We do it out of habit.

Similarly, while you're engrossed in a writing project, someone tells you the copy machine isn't working. You make a decision to call the repair service without much thought. Because you were busy with a more important project, you may have neglected to get all the information you needed before making the decision to call for repair, including checking to see that the machine is plugged in. Yet item number one of the trouble-shooting guide for the copy machine clearly states that you should check the power source before calling for service. Without such forethought, the stage is set for a potentially embarrassing and costly situation. The next time the copy machine fails to work, you'll probably take a moment to think through your decision before calling the repair service.

Postponement of Judgment

Whether you're making a decision, solving a problem or seeking opportunities, it's important to have as much information as possible at hand. The necessary information may be available through traditional sources — company manuals, files, the library, etc. — or from experience. You may need to use your imagination to think of more options.

Regardless of your thinking style, the guiding principle to follow when trying to come up with options is *Postponement of Judgment.* Don't decide what you're going to do until better options are available. By delaying, you increase the likelihood that you'll make the correct decision.

For example, suppose you have to pick a travel agency to handle your company's airline reservations. When you talk to the sales people from one agency, they offer you a 10 percent discount on air miles over 50,000 each month. If you accept this offer, you'll never know what other good deals are out there. However, when you decide to look at more options, you might find that the 50,000-mile offer is the industry standard and that a good deal is to get a rebate on hotel charges as well.

You can force yourself to postpone judgment by setting a minimum for the number of options you will look at. For example, you'll interview at least seven applicants for a job before deciding on the best one. Or you'll talk to no less than four vendors before making a buying decision.

Positive Judgment

When moving toward a goal, probably you'll need to make a number of decisions. In doing so, follow the principle of *Positive Judgment*, which means looking for the best alternatives.

By using Positive Judgment — selecting the best alternatives from among a sometimes overwhelming number — you will usually find three or four acceptable choices. This smaller group represents good alternatives from which you can select a best option. The remaining good alternatives can be saved for the future or serve as gateways to new opportunities. You used a lot of mental energy when you produced all those alternatives. While many of them can't be used this time, keep them handy so that when similar problems come up, you won't have to start from scratch. This strategy will help you be more productive.

For example, when planning to buy a new phone system for your office, you look at all the systems available. At decision time, you choose the one that best meets your needs instead of rejecting the others. This way, if the phone system you picked is no longer available, or if the vendor is no longer in business, then you still have a list of good phone systems.

Most people are familiar with the "process of elimination." When faced with a number of possibilities, some people choose by eliminating the worst alternative, then the next worst, then the next worst and so on, until they are left with the least worst of the alternatives. Some choice! By looking at the negative characteristics of the available options, and therefore labeling all other options as poor, the process of elimination is the opposite of Positive Judgment, which saves all available options for future use.

In general, adaptive thinkers are usually better at selecting alternatives than innovative thinkers because they enjoy direct, structured decisions. Innovative thinkers, on the other hand, like to look for options. Therefore, they need to use adaptive thinking tools and techniques to more quickly find successful results.

Personal Life	**Career**
Identify times in your personal life when you should: *1. Postpone Judgment* *2. Use Positive Judgment*	*Identify times in the workplace when you should:* *1. Postpone Judgment* *2. Use Positive Judgment*
The Thinking Box	
Identify times in problem-solving when you should: *1. Postpone Judgment* *2. Use Positive Judgment*	*Identify times in your personal growth when you should:* *1. Postpone Judgment* *2. Use Positive Judgment*
Problem-Solving	**Growth**

Friends and "Frustraters" Tool

When you apply thinking skills to a problem, you'll encounter situations, objects, events and people who will encourage you to think in new ways and help you in your endeavors. At the same time, you'll also discover situations, objects, events and people that intentionally or unintentionally get in the way. To improve your chances of success, you need to identify not only friends who will help you but also those around you who will and who should frustrate you. The Friends and "Frustraters" Tool provides a way to identify your helpers and hinderers.

Prepare a list of people, things, places and situations that can influence your thinking and encourage you to improve your abilities. Then prepare a second list of people, things, places and situations that are likely to hinder your development by tossing unwanted anchors in your direction. Depending on the circumstances, you may find that some items will appear on both lists. Figure 3-2 presents the Friends and Frustraters Tool.

FRIENDS AND FRUSTRATERS		
Thinking Tool, Technique, or Strategy:		
Friends		Frustraters
Who will help me?	**WHO**	Who will frustrate my progress?
What objects or events will help me?	**WHAT**	What objects or events will hinder my development?
What times are appropriate for rehearsal or practice?	**WHEN**	What times are inappropriate for practice or rehearsal?
What events or places are appropriate?	**WHERE**	What places or events are inappropriate?
Why would friends and associates help me?	**WHY**	Why would frustraters offer resistance to my success?
How can I be sure I am making progress?	**HOW**	How will I know when frustraters are slowing my progress?

Figure 3-2.

Figure 3-3 is an example of how you might complete the Friends and Frustraters Tool.

FRIENDS AND FRUSTRATERS		
Thinking Tool, Technique, or Strategy: *Postponing Judgment*		
Friends		Frustraters
Who will help me? *My sales manager, Kelly*	**WHO**	Who will frustrate my progress? *My co-worker, Pat*
What objects or events will help me? *Flipchart and easel*	**WHAT**	What objects or events will hinder my development? *When customers want delivery NOW*
What times are appropriate for rehearsal or practice? *Before meeting the customer*	**WHEN**	What times are inappropriate for practice or rehearsal? *When problems must be solved NOW*
What events or places are appropriate? *My office*	**WHERE**	What places or events are inappropriate? *Customers' places of business*
Why would friends and associates help me? *To increase company's profitability*	**WHY**	Why would frustraters offer resistance to my success? *Pat wants my job*
How can I be sure I am making progress? *When customers call with a problem and I have more than one answer to choose from*	**HOW**	How will I know when frustraters are slowing my progress? *When I fall back into old habits, such as jumping to conclusions*

Figure 3-3.

Practice or Rehearsal?

Throughout this book, you will see references to *practice* and *rehearsal*. Practice means repeatedly performing a drill or exercise to become good at a particular skill. The end result is usually a habit that allows you to perform an activity with little or no thought. Rehearsal means preparing for the performance or presentation of a particular activity. When you rehearse an activity, you plan for slight changes along the path to your desired results.

For example, a word processor learns keyboarding skills through extensive *practice* because it is essential that the motor skills involved become automatic. No thought should be needed to hit the right keys when speed is required. A sales representative *rehearses* a sales presentation. During the rehearsal, the sales rep anticipates questions and objections a customer may have so that the presentation is flexible.

You should *rehearse* rather than *practice* the tools and techniques you learn in ***The Power of Innovative Thinking***. Since no two situations are exactly the same, when you *rehearse* new tools and techniques, you learn how to adapt them to any challenges you meet.

Summary

In this chapter you learned about:

- The characteristics of reactive and proactive climates

- How strategies, techniques and tools differ

- The relationship among problem-solving, opportunity-seeking and decision-making

- How to avoid thinking "ruts"

- The principles of Postponement of Judgment and Positive Judgment

- The Friends and Frustraters Tool

- The differences between practice and rehearsal

4 THE RETHINKING MODEL

*"Inside each person there is a wonderful capacity to reflect
on the information that the various sense organs register,
and to direct and control these experiences."*
— *Mihaly Csikszentmihalyi*

Many companies do things in similar ways. For example:

- The Long-Range Planning Committee writes a broad statement that tells everyone where the company is headed

- Company leaders and corporate trainers motivate employees to do better

- The Research and Development Department creates new products

- Managers make decisions inside the company and customer service reps take care of problems outside the company

Similarly, as individuals, we may have followed the recommendations of time management experts and allocated blocks of time in our already busy schedule for:

- Long-range planning

- Personal development and motivational reading

- Listening to co-workers' suggestions on new ways to do things

- Making decisions on how to meet company goals and how to spend the rest of our time

We need to rethink how we work! The competition is getting stronger and smarter, our customers are more educated, and we are expected to do more with less. When we make decisions, we need to have a broader view of how we think and what happens as a result of our thinking. In the past, we learned to separate our tasks and responsibilities. Today, in order to work smarter, we need to learn how our thinking abilities are related and how to think our way to producing more with less.

THE RETHINKING MODEL

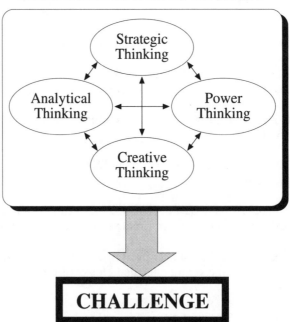

We can no longer say, "I'm going to plan for the future, so I'll think strategically." Or "The boss wants new ideas. I'll take a few minutes to think imaginatively." Each of the types of thinking skills is connected to the others, and when we are faced with a challenge, we need to employ all the types of thinking at the same time in order to be successful.

Types of Thinking Skills

Each of the thinking skills and specific tools and techniques will be discussed in the following chapters of *The Power of Innovative Thinking*. However, to whet your appetite, here's a preview of the four types of thinking skills:

- Strategic Thinking

- Power Thinking

- Creative Thinking

- Analytical Thinking

Strategic Thinking

Strategic thinking is the thinking skill we use when we are thinking about planning for the future. It connects today with tomorrow in an organized way and sets a course of action.

Power Thinking

Power thinking concentrates on the positive ingredients of any situation and helps us get around barriers on our way to planning for the future and making correct decisions.

Creative Thinking

Creative thinking gives us a way to look at the future and solutions from a fresh angle. It is a thinking skill that will get us out of the always-thinking-the same-way rut.

Analytical Thinking

Analytical thinking is necessary for us to stay organized while we look for the answers that will make us successful.

Connecting the Types of Thinking

Since the different types of thinking skills work together to make "right" decisions, we need to be aware of them no matter what problem we are trying to solve.

For example, if we need to develop a long-range plan, our strategic thinking skills are needed to develop a plan of action. Power thinking skills will help us defeat negative roadblocks. Creative thinking skills give us many possible solutions, while analytical thinking skills help us come up with the best possible plan of action.

Summary

In this chapter, you learned the four types of thinking skills and how they are related. You also learned that it is necessary to use all four at one time. In the next chapter, you will learn in detail about strategic thinking and the tools and techniques to use.

5 STRATEGIC THINKING

*"Discovering what you want in life can be
facilitated by the process of setting goals."*
— *Shakti Gawain*

What Is Strategic Thinking?

"Strategic" means planning for the future, and "Strategic Thinking" is thinking about planning for the future. When you know *where* you're going, *why* you're going and *how* you're going to get there, you'll get there successfully — and strategic-thinking tools will give you the *where, why* and *how*. Successful people learn to use their thinking skills so that the "best laid schemes o' mice and men" will not go astray, but will lead to desired goals.

The Four Drivers of Strategic Thinking

To some people, strategic *planning* means to set a goal and go for it. When you know what makes strategic *thinking* happen, you can not only "go for it," you can successfully achieve your goals. The drivers of strategic thinking are:

- Vision

- Resources

- Values

- Assumptions — yours and your organization's

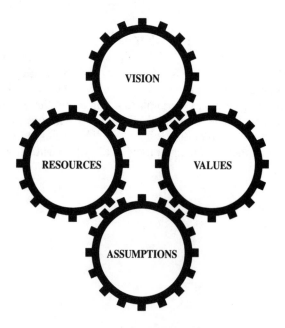

The Four Drivers of Strategic Thinking
Figure 5-1.

Vision

Your picture of the future may be very clear to you. You might see yourself obtaining a tangible asset — a new company car. It might even be something you can't see, feel or touch, such as high employee morale. You need to state your vision in clear, concise terms that you can measure so you can tell when it has become a reality. Good physical health is a marvelous goal; however, you need a way to know when you are in good physical health. For example, you might say that you are in good physical health when you can run 2 miles in 10 minutes, do 50 sit-ups or maintain your ideal weight for three months.

Case Study: 5-1.

Steve senses frustration and a poor attitude among the people in his department. He knows that something needs to change, so he envisions his department as a place with high employee morale. His mental picture includes smiling faces, friendly people having a good time and everyone willing to go that extra mile to keep customers happy.

While Steve's vision is very clear to him, the vision is difficult to attain because he hasn't stated it in terms that can be easily measured. Steve needs to include a standard that will tell him and those in his department when morale has improved. For example, he might include the following in his vision statement: no tardy employees during the next month, 100 percent participation in the company picnic or a five percent increase in the productivity and quality of his product with no customer complaints.

Your vision gives you direction. It needs to be stated so that others will understand the goal or the plan. A fuzzy cloud wandering through the sky without a solid border will break up and disappear. Your vision needs to be contained before you can grab it.

Resources

The resources available to you also help drive your thinking. The resources could include

- *Money.* Is money available so you can get to your vision? Is money in the budget? Can you add it to the budget? Are there other sources for the money?

45

- *Time.* Is there enough time to reach your goal? Can you, your associates or employees accomplish the vision without wasting time?

- *People.* Are there enough people available to make the plan happen? Are people willing to work on the plan?

- *Equipment.* Do you have the necessary equipment to work on and achieve the plan? Does the vision require updating or purchasing new equipment?

- *Skills.* Do you, your co-workers or employees have the necessary knowledge and training to work toward and reach the vision? How much training will people need?

All of these factors need to be looked at before you can move toward your vision. Strategically looking at these resources expands your thinking and helps you move from a rut to an opportunity.

Case Study: 5-2.

Mary is in charge of the medical claims department for a growing corporation. She supervises four employees who can process 1,000 claims with a turnaround time of eight days. Because the corporation is growing, Mary sees the need for processing 2,000 claims with a turnaround time of five days by the end of the year.

Mary's vision is clearly stated. Now she needs to examine her resources.

- Is there enough money in this year's budget to handle additional costs? Will there be enough money in next year's budget? What can she do to make sure there is enough money? (Resource: *Money*)

- Is one year enough time to accomplish her goal? (Resource: *Time*)

- Can the people in Mary's department handle the increased workload, or will she need to hire more people? (Resource: *People*)

- Is the present equipment capable of processing more claims, or will she need to purchase more equipment? What kind of equipment will be needed? (Resource: *Equipment*)

- Does Mary have the knowledge to make all the necessary decisions along the way? Can the other people in her department learn new skills before next year? Are there other people in the company who are willing to help? (Resource: *Skills*)

When you consider all the resources, you're thinking strategically. Each time you find a satisfactory answer to one of your questions, you've taken another step forward — and you did it by using your *strategic-thinking skills.*

Values

As we discussed earlier, values are located in frames, or frames of reference. Therefore, when you become strategic in your thinking, you need to examine your frames and anchors to see how your personal values — the "rightness" and "wrongness" — influence your vision and the resources.

Case Study: 5-3.

Michael is an adaptive thinker who enjoys making decisions quickly. His company supplies fresh fruits and vegetables to supermarkets and wants to add restaurants to its customer base. Michael was given the task of finding out if fruits and vegetables could be delivered to new restaurant customers on time. He had a mental picture of what his company wanted to do and thought it was a great idea. He immediately began to work out delivery schedules using ZIP codes. Proud of his ability to make sound decisions quickly, Michael presented the new delivery schedule to his manager within four hours.

Michael's values filtered out much of what was needed to do the job correctly. He was "hung up" or anchored on quick performance because his values encouraged him to make quick decisions. At the same time, his values prevented him from seeing the big picture. The task was broader than Michael's plan. Influenced solely by his values, Michael neglected to find out what resources, for example, were available — money for new trucks, delivery people, sales staff, advertising programs, etc. This knowledge would have made his plan better and more realistic.

When you are faced with a task that affects the future, you need to think about all the strategic-thinking drivers — vision, resources, values and assumptions — before writing the plan.

Assumptions

When you and I think about the future, we make assumptions. We might assume, for example, that all changes are good. We might assume that our company will continue to grow simply by selling more of our product. Or we might assume that the only way for our company to grow is to move into other markets or to add more products to our line. We might develop a plan and assume that everyone in our organization will buy into the plan.

Case Study: 5-4.

Ray was hired in 1977 by a large insurance company as a payroll clerk. He had the mechanical ability to fix manual typewriters and adding machines when they broke down, and even though it didn't fit his job description, he'd fix the broken machines, saving his company thousands of dollars by reducing the number of service calls. When management realized Ray's skills and abilities, they created a position for him and encouraged him to take advanced training in machine repair. He became very good at what he did and was the only one in the company who could fix the machines. Ray assumed that he would be set for life with the company. In 1985, the company installed electronic equipment. In 1986, Ray was without a job because of his incorrect assumption.

Because he was the expert, Ray assumed that his job would be there forever. When his skills were no longer required, Ray was no longer required. When using strategic thinking, you need to be sure that your assumptions are correct.

Engaging the Gears

The four drivers of strategic thinking are like four gears in a machine. All four gears must move together if strategic thinking is to work well. If one of the gears doesn't move, then strategic thinking will not occur. As with any machine, the gears need to be lubricated so they can move smoothly together. You need to know where the friction points are located and what kind of "oil" to use to prevent "burn-out."

Case Study: 5-5.

Laurie, the senior maintenance supervisor, was asked to write a long-range training program for all the plant maintenance people. The first thing Laurie did was to interview the company's management team members to find out why they wanted the training program and what results they expected. She then wrote a list of all the resources she thought she'd need and contacted the responsible managers and directors. The budget director told her how much money was in the budget. The training coordinator gave her a list of training rooms, instructors, and audio-visual equipment. She asked the shift supervisors what kind of training they thought everyone needed, both now and two years from now, and what were the best times to hold training sessions. She also found out what the maintenance workers thought would be the right kind of training. Rather than write down her own ideas about training, she took the time to find out what kind of training everyone wanted.

Do you think Laurie's way of putting together the training program will succeed? YES!!

- She has a clear understanding of the *vision*

- She knows what *resources* are available

- She has listened to how others *value* training

- Because of her talks with managers, supervisors and employees, Laurie has a good idea of their *assumptions* about the training program

49

Laurie's training program has yet to move forward because she took the time to use strategic thinking before doing the strategic planning. When Laurie begins writing the training program, she will do it efficiently and successfully. When you follow Laurie's example, you too will be successful.

Personal Life

Identify the drivers of strategic thinking in your personal life:
1. Vision
2. Resources
3. Values
4. Assumptions

Career

Identify the drivers of strategic thinking in your workplace:
1. Vision
2. Resources
3. Values
4. Assumptions

The Thinking Box

Identify the drivers of strategic thinking that influence how you solve problems:
1. Vision
2. Resources
3. Values
4. Assumptions

Problem-Solving

Identify the drivers of strategic thinking that influence your personal and career growth:
1. Vision
2. Resources
3. Values
4. Assumptions

Growth

Connecting Strategic Thinking with Strategic Planning

When you actually prepare a strategic plan, you can be assured of success if you use the four drivers of strategic thinking to examine each step of the planning process. The first couple of times you use this technique, it will take you longer than more traditional reactive thinking. The results, however, will be well worth your time investment. The Strategic-Thinking/Planning Checklist will help you stay on track and prompt you to use your thinking skills at each planning step. You will keep your strategic plan and your strategic thinking connected when you complete the checklist.

Strategic-Thinking/Planning Checklist

Strategic-Planning Steps	Strategic-Thinking Drivers	
1. Determine the purpose	Vision	
	Resources	
	Values	
	Assumptions	
2. Establish a vision	Vision	
	Resources	
	Values	
	Assumptions	
3. Assess the external environment	Vision	
	Resources	
	Values	
	Assumptions	
4. Assess the internal environment	Vision	
	Resources	
	Values	
	Assumptions	
5. Establish long-range objectives	Vision	
	Resources	
	Values	
	Assumptions	

Strategic-Planning Steps	Strategic-Thinking Drivers	
6. Establish short-range objectives	Vision	
	Resources	
	Values	
	Assumptions	
7. Prioritize objectives	Vision	
	Resources	
	Values	
	Assumptions	
8. Analyze objectives in terms of who will help and what obstacles may be encountered	Vision	
	Resources	
	Values	
	Assumptions	
9. Develop step-by-step plans for reaching objectives	Vision	
	Resources	
	Values	
	Assumptions	
10. Monitor the progress of your plans	Vision	
	Resources	
	Values	
	Assumptions	

Anchoring Tools

There are tools you can use to build an anchor for strategic thinking. When you create an anchor, you establish a starting point or place from which to do your thinking. Sometimes the problem you're about to tackle is not clearly defined. To help you solve the problem properly, you need to find the *real* problem. You can do so by using three anchoring tools: "Why? x 5," the "Care-Its" and the Reality-to-Ideal Ladder.

"Why? x 5" Tool

The "Why? x 5" Tool will move you from something that is unclear to something that is concrete. After you have asked "Why?" five times, you will be able to identify a specific anchoring point.

Case Study: 5-6.

Jason: *I need a new service truck!*

Wendy: *Why do you need a new service truck?*

Jason: *The truck stops running every time it rains.*

Wendy: *Why does it stop running when it rains?*

Jason: *Well, the service foreman thought that the ignition wires get wet.*

Wendy: *Why do the wires get wet?*

Jason: *Because the insulation is cracked.*

Wendy: *Why is the insulation cracked?*

Jason: *Because the wires are old.*

Wendy: *Why would you drive a truck with old ignition wires?*

Jason: *I don't have time to get them replaced.*

Jason wants a new truck simply because the ignition wires need to be replaced! When you rephrase what the other person has said and reflect it back to him in the form of a "Why?" question, you get to the meat of the problem. The questioning process moves from a general statement to a specific statement.

Sometimes five "Why?s" aren't necessary. You may be able to find the real problem after only two or three questions.

Case Study: 5-7.

> Betsy: *My computer isn't working right!*
>
> Bryce: *Why isn't it working right?*
>
> Betsy: *When I try to get into the database of employees, it asks for my password. I enter my name and the screen goes blank.*
>
> Bryce: *Why do you enter your name?*
>
> Betsy: *Because I don't have a password.*
>
> Bryce: *Why don't you have a password?*
>
> Betsy: *Because access to the database is limited to only a few people.*

The "Why? x 5" tool requires you to listen carefully to the other person. Between the first and fifth "Why?," a statement emerges that will point out the anchor. We can solve Jason's problem, not by buying a new truck, but by figuring out how he can make time to get the ignition wires replaced. Similarly, Betsy's problem is not with the computer. Instead, she needs to find another source from which to get her information or obtain a password.

The "Care-Its" Tool

When you need to anchor yourself in values, you can use the "Care-Its" tool. With this tool, you can discover how people's values are related. It will let you use your thinking skills to look through filters that may interfere with your thinking. The "Care-Its" tool asks you to answer three questions. Look at your answers and find values that are the same and values that are different. You can use this information to build on the similarities and bring the differences together.

The "Care-Its" Tool

WHAT DOES MY ORGANIZATION REALLY CARE ABOUT?	WHAT DO MY CUSTOMERS REALLY CARE ABOUT?	WHAT DO I REALLY CARE ABOUT?

For example, you might find that your organization, your customers and you all really care about serving the community. Since all three parts of the tool have the same "Care-It," you can use this as an anchor. As a result, your thinking can be concentrated on how to involve your organization and customers in a fund-raising event for needy children.

On the other hand, when you see differences in values, you may need to develop a plan to bring people's values closer together. Say, for instance, that your organization really cares about increasing profits, your customers really care about reducing costs, while you care about making a decent wage. The "Care-Its" seem to be heading in opposite directions. To bring them closer together, you might think of ways by which your organization can help customers reduce costs and build a base of loyal customers who will continue to buy from your organization. Increased profits, in turn, may mean a raise for you. Incidentally, some insurance companies are doing this now. Instead of just selling insurance, they help clients reduce risks so they can keep their insurance premiums low.

The Reality-to-Ideal Ladder

This tool can be fun because you get a chance to play with a magic wand that lets you have anything you want. Use your imagination! Wave your magic wand and choose your ideal goal. At the top of the ladder, write a description of your ideal goal. At the bottom of the ladder, write a description of the way things really are. Start with the first rung and write one thing that needs to change so you can get closer to the top. On the next rung, list one more thing that needs changing, and so on up the ladder. If the ideal is not too far from reality, you can take some rungs out. If the ideal is far away from reality, add as many rungs as you need.

Each rung of the ladder becomes an anchor for steps — objectives — that lead to your ideal goal. Each rung forces you to think through barriers that may have kept you from moving toward your ideal goal.

Reality-to-Ideal Ladder

Figure 5-2.

For example, suppose your ideal goal is to get a college degree in marketing. In reality, you have about three semesters of college credits. The top rung would read, "Get my degree." The bottom rung on the Reality-to-Ideal Ladder might be labeled "How many more courses do I need?" The next rung up could be labeled, "When can I take the courses I need?" The third rung, "What's available to help me pay tuition?" The last rung before the top could read, "When do I register?" When you have answers to your questions, you have moved closer to your ideal goal.

Personal Life

Identify situations in your personal life when you will use these tools:
- *"Why? x 5"*
- *"Care-Its"*
- *Reality-to-Ideal Ladder*

Career

Identify a situation in your work life when you will use these tools:
- *"Why? x 5"*
- *"Care-Its"*
- *Reality-to-Ideal Ladder*

The Thinking Box

Identify how you will use each of the strategic thinking tools to help you solve problems:
- *"Why? x 5"*
- *"Care-Its"*
- *Reality-to-Ideal Ladder*

Problem-Solving

Identify how you will use each of the strategic thinking tools to help you grow personally and professionally:
- *"Why? x 5"*
- *"Care-Its"*
- *Reality-to-Ideal Ladder*

Growth

Summary

In this chapter, you learned about:

- Strategic thinking

- The four drivers of strategic thinking

- Vision

- Resources

- Values

- Assumptions

- Connecting strategic thinking with strategic planning

- Anchoring tools

- "Why? x 5" tool

- "Care-Its" tool

- Reality-to-Ideal Ladder

Strategic thinking lets you think about planning long-range goals. Using the drivers of strategic thinking gives you a chance to "think" rather than "feel" when you are setting goals. Anchoring tools help you avoid the pitfalls otherwise often placed before you by your filters. When you use the tools presented in this chapter, you are more likely to achieve your long-range plans.

6 POWER THINKING

"If you expect the worst, you'll get the worst,
and if you expect the best, you'll get the best."
— *Norman Vincent Peale*

Power thinking may be considered a new Olympic event in which competitors think through weighty problems with ease. While you may not win a gold medal at power thinking, you can be successful when you learn how to use the power-thinking tools and techniques that will be discussed in this chapter.

What Is Power?

"Power" is being able to influence people or situations. It's not reserved only for people in authority or those with the biggest stick. Power is something we all have and should be seen as neither good nor bad. When we abuse power, it is bad; but when we use power to turn a vision into a reality, it is good.

The amount of power or influence you have is determined by how much power other people let you have. For example, people are cheated by con-artists because they accept the power that the swindlers claim they have. If you tell someone to do something and she does it, you have power. If she doesn't do it, you don't have power.

Other types of power come from a person's job title, skills or knowledge, which we will briefly look at before going into the specifics of power thinking.

Job Title

The president of a corporation is seen by many as having a lot of power. Teachers are seen as having power in the classroom. Similarly, if you are a shift supervisor, you have power over the people on your shift; however, you probably don't have power over people on another shift or in another department. The power you have goes with the job title. Because people expect you to act in a certain way, given your title, it is important for you to have strong power-thinking skills to capitalize on this power. When you do, people will listen to you and follow your lead.

Skills and Knowledge

If you are good at what you do or know more than others about a certain job, you have the potential for a lot of power. How you use your skills and knowledge will determine how much power you have. For example, the "show-off" or braggart has very little power because people dislike this kind of behavior. Instead, people prefer to find out for themselves how much you know.

Case Study: 6-1.

Debbie graduated at the top of her class with a degree in medical office skills from a local junior college. The office manager of a medical clinic was impressed with her skills and hired her for general office work. The office manager told Debbie that, because of her excellent school record, she would add a lot to the office and that she looked forward to learning the new things that Debbie brought with her. Debbie was confident about her ability to handle almost any task given to her and showed initiative. When she saw something that needed doing, she did it. She had the potential for promotion and looked forward to regular pay raises. However, when other people in the office asked the office manager for advice or instructions, Debbie would often butt into the conversations. She knew what was supposed to be done and wanted everyone else to know she knew it. As a result, co-workers began closing the office manager's door when they had questions. They avoided Debbie and didn't accept her knowledge as power.

Debbie had the potential to assume a lot of power in the office; however, she chose to grab power from the office manager and her co-workers by telling everyone how much she knew rather than using her knowledge for the good of the office. People don't care how much you know until they know how much you care. If people first had the chance to know how much Debbie cared about sharing her knowledge, then they might have cared about how much she knew.

When you use your skills and knowledge so that other people benefit, you have true power. People respect your talents and usually look forward to learning something from you. You have the power to influence their decisions.

What Is Power Thinking?

"Power thinking" is thinking about how to create successes by using your positive-thinking abilities and developing your self-esteem. In other words, power thinking means using your power-thinking skills to achieve your goals. Power thinking is related to positive thinking and self-esteem because you are confident you can reach your goals. When you use positive thinking, you are strengthening your power-thinking skills.

Steps to Power Thinking

In order to influence people and situations, you need to use your power-thinking skills. In a given situation, use the following steps to ensure that you are using power thinking:

1. Recognize what's right

2. Go with the positive

3. Keep your eye on the negative

4. Turn the negative into a positive

The emphasis in power thinking is on using a positive approach in every situation. This does not mean you should just ignore the negatives — this can be disastrous. Acknowledge their presence, and do what you can to change negatives into positives.

When you take a positive approach, you can influence people and situations. Your power-thinking skills will keep you on track and reward you with successful results.

The ABCs of Power Thinking

The ABCs of power thinking are **A**ction, **B**enefit and **C**ommitment. When you follow the guidelines for developing your power-thinking skills presented below, you can make good decisions and successfully reach your goals.

Action

To develop your power-thinking skills, you need to act. The first step is to prepare an improvement plan that will make you a better power thinker. Remember the four drivers of strategic thinking from Chapter 3 — Vision, Resources, Values and Assumptions? Improving your power-thinking skills means setting up a long-range plan for self-improvement.

- Create a *vision* of yourself using your power-thinking skills

- Determine the *resources* available to you

- Look at your *values* to see if they line up with your vision

- Think about your *assumptions* and your organization's *assumptions*

To get started, you might want to complete the following inventory. Be specific about your vision. Your statements should be clear and concise so that you will know when you have accomplished your vision. Find a friend or two whom you can trust, and ask them to help you complete some of the information.

You may need to reexamine your filters (subconscious, survival and social) to see if they are helping you or preventing you from working in a positive attitude frame. Maybe certain experiences have created a negative anchor. For instance, if you hated English grammar in high school, every time someone helps you with your writing skills, you get angry. When you consciously identify the anchor, you can use power-thinking tools to remove the anchor or change it to a positive anchor.

MY POWER-THINKING IMPROVEMENT PLAN

Vision	Resources	Values	Assumptions
I see myself developing my power-thinking skills by: *1. Concentrating on the positive approach* *2. Using words that are positive* *3. (Continue with your own visions of what you will do to improve your power-thinking skills)*			Mine: - - - - - - - - - - Theirs:

Case Study: 6-2.

Carlos is a good worker and is liked by his co-workers and his supervisor; however, whenever he gets a message to call his boss, he puts it off until the last possible minute, thinking he has done something wrong or that the boss has bad news for him. Carlos has had bad experiences at his previous two jobs. At the last job, the boss left a message for Carlos to stop in for a talk. When Carlos went to see his boss, he was told that the company was going out of business and that his job no longer existed. At another job, his boss was overbearing and blamed Carlos for mistakes that other workers had made.

When Carlos becomes aware of his negative anchor, he can see it is a result of bad experiences. He can consciously respond to his boss's request more quickly and neutrally. "See the boss" can mean good news too.

You can build a positive attitude frame by creating positive anchors that focus on what's good about a situation.

Benefit

When you use your power-thinking skills, you have a clear idea of how your actions will benefit you and the people you work with. Doing something merely for the sake of doing it may have an accidental benefit; however, effective power thinkers have a purpose for doing something.

Case Study: 6-3.

Nick was recently promoted to Team Supervisor. He knew he had a lot to learn if he was to do a good job, so he began to read everything he could on how to supervise people.

Nick is learning how to think like a supervisor. He knows his increased knowledge will benefit him and his company. He is taking action so all will benefit.

Commitment

Power thinking requires a commitment — a commitment to act in a positive way so that the greatest number of people will benefit. When you decide to improve your power-thinking skills, you are making a commitment of your time and energy. You are saying that you will act in a way that you and others will benefit from. By acting on the visions in your Power-Thinking Improvement Plan that require the least amount of effort, you are taking the first step toward a larger commitment. And after you complete the first few steps, the rest become easier.

Positive Thinking

Positive thinking is usually done by people who have a positive attitude. We can't see an "attitude," but we can see how people behave and hear the things they say. For example, "Yes!!" gives you a different message than "Yeah, sure ...well, maybe." Or one of your employees promises to get to work on time, yet shows up late the next day. The words and actions people use give you an idea of their attitude. While we can't see how a person thinks, we can see the actions and hear the words associated with a positive attitude.

The positive attitude is a frame in which positive thinkers work. When you use positive thinking as an anchor inside the positive attitude frame, you have put together a powerful strategy — a strategy that will lead to success for you, your co-workers, and your organization.

Thomas Edison, who holds the record for patented inventions, had over 6,000 failures before finding the right material for the electric light filament. As he was working on his invention, he kept going even though he met with failure many times. To Edison, those failures were not failures — they were *discoveries*. He was getting closer to the right filament because he had discovered another material that didn't work! Edison was "framed" in a positive attitude and "anchored" with positive-thinking behaviors — those behaviors that looked for the good in apparent failures.

Barriers to Positive Thinking

In the workplace, we encounter barriers that keep positive thinking from taking place. When these barriers are present, we automatically react to situations without thinking about the poor logic in our responses.

Definitive: *"If I'm not a winner, I'm a loser."* This barrier allows only for "right" or "wrong" responses. The person thinks that there are only two reactions and is unable to see that a less-than-perfect answer can also be "right."

- **Positive-Thinking Response:** "I may not be a winner, but I sure learned a lot."

Minimization: *"It was no big thing. I was just lucky."* It's OK to "blow your own horn" once in a while and take credit for your accomplishments.

- **Positive-Thinking Response:** "I didn't realize it was that important. Thank you for the kind words."

Negatives can't/positives don't: *"Sure, I did OK this time, but . . . ."* Positive thinkers rarely keep score when it comes to successes and failures.

- **Positive-Thinking Response:** "I did OK this time. It shows me that I'm capable."

Comparison: *"Compared to Pat, I'm nothing."* Each of us is different. Each of us has strong points and weak points.

- **Positive-Thinking Response:** "Pat sets a good example for us to follow."

Incorrect assumptions: *"I know you're thinking the worst."* We may try to read other people's minds and assume their response will be negative.

- **Positive-Thinking Response:** "What are you thinking?"

Fortune teller: *"No use even trying. I know what's going to happen."* If we expect the worst, we'll get the worst. Positive thinkers think the best will happen.

- **Positive-Thinking Response:** "I'll give it a shot. We'll succeed this time."

Critics are always right: *"They're right. I do act immature."* Critics express opinions, and often the opinions are not based on fact. Positive thinkers consider the source and think through the opinion.

- **Positive-Thinking Response:** "In their eyes, I may be immature. Everyone else thought my actions led to the correct decision."

Personalization: *"He didn't like my report; therefore, he doesn't like me."* Just because the result of our efforts is less than perfect, it doesn't mean that people have the same feelings about us. We all have made incorrect decisions during our careers, and we have survived.

- **Positive-Thinking Response:** "He didn't like the report, but he still respects my judgment."

I feel; therefore, I am: *"I feel stupid; therefore, I am stupid."* Instead of using our thinking skills, we let our emotions create a barrier for us. This incorrect logic lets our emotions rule over our thinking ability.

- **Positive-Thinking Response:** "That was a dumb thing to do. I need to think before I act the next time."

The "Shoulda's:" *"You should always keep your desk neat and clean."* The "shoulda's" come from our value filters. We may have been taught that cleanliness is important. While it may be important to personal hygiene, there may be more important things than cleanliness when it comes to our desk and work priorities.

- **Positive-Thinking Response:** "If I want to succeed, I need to continually adjust my priorities."

Do some of the barriers sound familiar? Make a check mark next to them so you know which ones you need to work on. When you identify the barriers that are familiar to you, you have taken the first step on the road to improving your power-thinking skills.

Personal Life
What barriers to positive thinking in my personal life do I need to eliminate?

Career
What barriers to positive thinking do I need to eliminate in my workplace?

The Thinking Box

What barriers to positive thinking prevent me from solving problems effectively?

Problem-Solving

What barriers to positive thinking hurt my personal and professional growth?

Growth

Changing Negative Patterns to Positive-Thinking Anchors

When we are anchored in negative patterns, we approach situations from the wrong side. For example, when a job opens up that leads to a promotion, you can work toward that promotion in one of two ways. If you use a negative anchor, you'll think of all the reasons why you won't get the promotion. When you build a positive anchor, you'll think of all the things you can do to get promoted.

Karl Wallenda, the famous tight-rope walker, fell to his death in 1978. When his wife was interviewed later, she said she had noticed a change in Karl before his fatal accident. He had begun to think about not falling, whereas in his previous attempts, he thought about getting to the other side. He had changed his positive anchor into a negative anchor — with disastrous results.

When we build positive-thinking anchors, we build starting points for using our positive-thinking skills that lead to success.

- *From Adversity to Opportunity.* Adversity is seen by some as disaster, misfortune or hardship. Opportunity, on the other hand, can be seen as a chance or an opening for something better. When faced with what appears to be a failure, the positive thinker adjusts toward the positive and builds an anchor on the positive points.

Case Study: 6-4.

At the age of 40, Rusty, a parts designer for the aerospace industry, was laid off because of the reduction in military spending. He secretly thanked his previous employer for helping him make a decision that he had been thinking about for a long time. Rather than look upon his job loss as an adversity, he jumped at a chance to do something he had always wanted to do — help others. He is now a licensed practical nurse and is looking forward to becoming a registered nurse.

Rusty found a way to work toward his vision. Not wanting to quit his job because he'd lose steady income, his thoughts of becoming a nurse were only a dream until he turned adversity into opportunity.

When you anchor yourself in opportunity, the number of times you face adversity will decrease. And when you seek opportunities, your positive-thinking skills become stronger.

- *From Negative Beliefs to Positive Alternatives.* When we are anchored in negative beliefs, we fail to see the positive alternatives in situations. Our negative anchor magnifies the failure in a situation. By contrast, when you look for positive alternatives, you learn from failure and build on the things that you have accomplished.

Case Study: 6-5.

Jamie was a likable guy who believed that meetings were a waste of time and resented having to work with strangers on the newly organized quality team. At the first meeting of the quality team, Jamie listened to the others, but didn't take part in any of the discussions. He met people he didn't know from other departments who were excited about the work of the team. At future meetings, they asked Jamie questions about the work that went on in his department. He was good at his job, and the other team members respected his opinion. Jamie began to look forward to the meetings. He liked the people on his team, and they saw him as a useful member. When a supervisory position opened up in another department, one team member suggested that Jamie apply for the promotion.

In the beginning, Jamie's negative belief about meetings produced an anchor that could have prevented him from being a valuable member of the quality team. When Jamie began to see the benefits of the meetings, he was rewarded — he increased his opportunity for promotion and increased his circle of friends.

Negative beliefs close the door on future success. Positive beliefs lead to success.

- *From Reactive to Proactive.* Instead of anchoring yourself in a reactive climate, think proactive. When faced with a problem, use your strategic-thinking skills to look for answers that not only solve the immediate problem, but also prevent the problem from happening in the future. At least you'll be prepared to take on future problems when they occur.

Case Study: 6-6.

Bill was in charge of the shipping department for a manufacturer of industrial machinery. He knew when orders were scheduled for completion and always notified the trucking company in plenty of time to arrange for pick up and delivery. On the day he had several important shipments ready for pick up, the trucking industry went on strike. Bill grabbed the telephone book and began looking for other ways to ship the machinery.

If Bill had been proactive instead of reactive, he would have had other shipping alternatives planned. By preparing for the worst, Bill could very easily have handled any situation that came his way. Plan for the worst, and work toward the best.

When we are anchored in a proactive climate, we prepare for future problems. If you are CPR-trained, you have learned a skill that you hope you will never have to use. Learning how to perform CPR is being proactive. You are prepared for the future so that you can work toward successful results when the situation arises.

- *From a Negative Energizer to the First Action Step.* When faced with a can't-be-done situation, some people spend a lot of energy worrying about defeat — "If I don't succeed, something bad will happen." Turn that negative energy into the first action step. "What can I do that will turn this situation around and lead to success?" When the underdog football team wins, people ask, "How did they do it?" The usual response is, "One play at a time." Being the underdog can be a great motivator.

Case Study: 6-7.

Susan was transferred to another branch office and promoted to office supervisor. When she arrived at her new office, the place was in a shambles — files were everywhere, employees were doing each other's work, the telephone system was outdated and the office staff was "putting out fires" instead of serving customers. Rather than panic, Susan surveyed the situation and used her strategic-thinking skills to develop a plan to get things in shape. She identified the first step toward getting things on the right track — everyone would concentrate on customer service while she put out the fires. Susan put her energies into making the office a smooth-running operation by using her power-thinking skills.

Susan could have accepted the negative situation and let things continue as they were. Instead, she chose to become anchored with the first action step.

Ray Kroc didn't decide 40 years ago that he was going to open a fast-food restaurant in Moscow. He started by perfecting a milk shake machine used by the McDonald brothers in California. The McDonald's Corporation followed a well-thought-out first step before creating a worldwide demand for its fast foods.

To succeed at a seemingly enormous task, identify the first step so that you can create a starting point — a positive anchor. Place your energies into completing the first step, and then each step that follows until you reach your goal successfully.

Self-Esteem

Power thinking is also affected by your own self-esteem. In order to maximize your power-thinking skills, you need to be positive about yourself and your abilities. Self-esteem is determined by your self-expectations and the expectations of other people. How you see yourself and the confidence you have in your ability to be successful will influence your power-thinking skills.

When we see ourselves as successful, we will be successful. The power of positive mental pictures has been recognized for a long time. Athletes and public speakers are some of the people who practice their skills with positive mental images of success. Studies now underway are showing that basketball players who add mental pictures of scoring baskets to real practice actually score more baskets than the players who only practice making baskets. Public speakers are learning to overcome stage fright by rehearsing in front of imaginary audiences. The audience is imagined as excited and glad to hear the presentation. When the mental rehearsal is finished, the speaker receives an imaginary standing ovation.

Athletes are developing the expectations they have of themselves. Public speakers are building on what other people expect as well as their own expectations. When you create mental pictures of success, you develop positive expectations in yourself and in others. Creating positive expectations will allow you to unleash the force of your power-thinking skills.

Improving Self-Esteem with Successes

One way you can improve your self-esteem is to recognize your past successes. When you see what you have done, you are telling yourself that you are good, that you can be successful. You are creating positive expectations for yourself.

Use the following plan to look at the past and improve on your self-esteem. In the first column, list those things in your personal life and career that you can honestly say were successes. It might be raising your children, selling $1,000,000 in real estate, or getting to work each day on time. In the second column, list those things that you see as failures — getting a speeding ticket, missing out on that last promotion or losing that sale last week to a competitor.

You can start by listing one or two of your successes and failures, or you can dig right in and list a whole bunch of them. The important thing is to be able to recognize the success or failure. In the third column, identify some part of the item in the failure column that was a success. To complete this column, you may have to use the positive-thinking tools you just learned. Chances are, when those failures occurred, you had not yet created positive-thinking anchors. What's done is done, and the power thinker knows that the past is filled with good learning experiences! Here is an opportunity to apply those tools in a nonthreatening way.

The plan includes an example to help get you started.

A LOOK AT MY SUCCESSES

Successes	Failures	NEW SUCCESSES!!!
.	*I lost the sale of 100 gallons of sealer to Star Track Enterprises.*	*1. I met the purchasing manager, Dennis.* *2. I discovered they will need weatherproof paint for their new outdoor track next month.*

When you find success in failure, your self-esteem is boosted, and you can find opportunities that you didn't know existed. Each failure can lead to success if you use the proper framing tools and create positive-thinking anchors.

Control of your self-esteem means that your self-expectations will be realistic and easily acquired. You will understand that the expectations others have of you are less important. Then you can begin to show others that you are using your power-thinking skills to be successful.

Summary

In this chapter, you learned about power thinking and what it takes to move a situation to success. To develop your power-thinking skills, you need to:

- Understand the role of positive thinking

- Recognize barriers to positive thinking

- Change negative patterns into positive-thinking anchors

You also learned how self-esteem influences power thinking, and you discovered how to improve your self-esteem by looking at your successes.

The ABCs of power thinking are action, benefit and commitment. You learned that commitment to a long-range improvement plan is important.

Good luck on the road to building your power-thinking skills, to becoming all you are capable of becoming!

7 CREATIVE THINKING

*"Real constructive mental power lies in
the creative thought that shapes your destiny."*
— *Laurence J. Peter*

What Is Creative Thinking?

"Creative thinking" is using your thinking skills to make new and useful connections — creative solutions from information you already know. Aristotle said that something comes from something, and that is the purpose of creative thinking — to make something new, unique or different out of something old.

All people are creative, but in different ways. You may be creative when it comes to putting words on paper while an associate is creative in designing buildings. Once you recognize that you are creative, you can apply your thinking skills to come up with new and useful solutions to problems.

The Creative Process

We often think of a creative solution as something that just happens. In fact, the opposite is true. The mental process that gives us creative answers happens in four stages:

1. Getting Ready

2. Mulling It Over

3. The AHA!

4. Checking It Out

Getting Ready

To exercise your creative thinking, you need to get ready to look for new connections:

- Recognize when there is an opportunity for creative answers

- Understand the problem or the opportunity for future problems to occur

- Gather information about the problem

For example, suppose you work for a plumbing supply company that wants to keep dirt from collecting in pipes. You need to find out if there is already a problem or if you need to prevent a problem. You look for all possible information. You might interview workers in the field to see what has been done in the past. Under what conditions do pipes collect dirt? Have other companies prepared for the same problem?

The information gathered can be facts or feelings. When you are in control of your thinking, it is OK to recognize feelings and emotions. Experienced workers often have a gut feeling about a situation. Their intuition about the rightness or wrongness of a situation comes from years of working at their job.

Mulling It Over

This stage in the creative process can be the most frustrating. In a reactive climate where time is usually important, getting away from the problem to mull it over is often difficult because it takes time. However, scientists have proven that the best solutions occur after we take a mental break from the problem. In other words, let the problem and all the information germinate in your mind for a while.

The subconscious mind has ways of connecting unrelated information. Some of the tools you will learn later in this chapter speed up this stage and enable you to use your conscious mind to make new and useful connections.

The AHA!

The third stage in the creative process that leads to new and useful answers is the AHA! Here we connect information that has been stored in our memory, and the solution we are looking for comes to us like a flash of light! It can occur within a few minutes after meeting the problem, or it may be longer.

In Chapter 1 of *The Power of Innovative Thinking*, you learned about communicating in the AHA Zone. That is when you communicate with others about information that you didn't know you knew. When you realize you know more than you thought you did, you have a feeling similar to the AHA.

We have all experienced this step. Can't remember someone's name? And when you walk away, or some days later, for no reason the name comes to you — in a flash. Or you solve a problem right away, and afterwards you think of a better solution.

Checking It Out

When the solution comes to us, we need to check it out to see if it will really work. Some solutions are too costly or impractical. Some solutions are so new and different that the technology needed is not yet available.

For example, safety on our interstate highways is a problem. One solution to improving safety is to place magnetic fields under the pavement and equip cars so that they can ride on the magnetic field — all in the same lane and at the same speed. The technology is available; however, the cost of putting this system into place is extremely high.

Business travelers face another problem — the time spent in traveling. Wouldn't it be nice if travelers could step into a capsule and instantly be transported from New York City to Los Angeles? Or from your home to a vacation spot? While this may be a great solution to travel problems, the technology is not yet available.

Solutions may be good ones, but they need to be examined before we can use them. If none of the solutions work, then we gather more information and look for other solutions.

Guidelines for Creative Thinking

Even if your workplace is not representative of a creative climate, you can control your creative thinking skills and offer others creative solutions. The basic procedure in creative thinking is to allow your thoughts to diverge — to go in many different directions. When you do what you've always done, you get the "same old" results. When you follow the guidelines for creative thinking, you'll get something new and get out of the rut.

Innovative thinkers enjoy divergent thinking because they can let their minds go anyplace. Sometimes they think inside the paradigm, sometimes outside the paradigm. Adaptive thinkers are also creative thinkers. Because they would rather find an immediate answer, adaptive thinkers usually rely on creative-thinking tools more than innovative thinkers.

The four basic guidelines for increasing your divergent thinking are:

- Postpone judgment

- Generate large numbers of ideas

- Accept the ridiculous

- Form new links

Postpone Judgment

Each of the four guidelines is important; however, unless you delay judging your ideas and solutions, the other guidelines cannot operate. When you postpone judgment as each idea is generated, you can think of twice as many ideas in the same amount of time. Also, some people are more willing to throw in ideas if they know they won't be judged right away. Finally, when you build lists of many potential solutions, you are more likely to come up with the right ones.

It may be hard for you to get others to refrain from judging each idea as it is presented. This is where you need to use your power-thinking tools to your advantage. Influence others to follow your lead when they need to make decisions. For example, if you know that others want new answers, use the value they place on newness to sell them on postponing judgment. You can say, for instance, "You said you wanted some new suggestions. Well, do I have some for you!" Or maybe they're bored with the problem-solving process. When you use creative-thinking tools, you will create a fun atmosphere on the way to the correct solution, and others will see how important it is to postpone judgment.

Generate Large Numbers of Ideas

It has been proven that the best solutions to problems come only after many solutions have been generated. When you use your creative-thinking skills, make a conscious effort to look for as many ideas as you can. Quantity breeds quality. The more ideas you can think of, the greater the likelihood of finding a gold nugget.

When you are shooting for large quantities, 50 is not an unreasonable number to start with. For example, as an exercise in problem-solving, a group of Air Force personnel were asked to solve a problem for which there was already an answer. In the early 1950s, it was feared that long-distance telephone lines in the state of Washington would break because ice crystals had formed along hundreds of miles of long-distance wire. The Air Force people were asked to find a solution to this problem. If they had stopped after generating 35 solutions, they would not have found the correct answer. Their 36th solution turned out to be the way the problem had been solved.

When you are coming up with many solutions, the first third tend to be the usual answers. The second third are usually from outer space, while the final third usually contain the most creative and best solutions — ones that are new and useful.

(Incidentally, the long-distance telephone company flew helicopters over the wires. The down draft from the helicopter blades shook the ice off the wires. Why didn't Air Force people think of that first?!)

Accept the Ridiculous

When you accept only logical ideas or solutions, you never stretch your imagination. You need to get through the ridiculous solutions before you can hit upon one that may be connected to reality. Ridiculous ideas are outside the business-as-usual rut and lead you to think of solutions that are unique or different.

When asked to think of many uses for a bathtub, a group of people came up with over 100 ideas in only 15 minutes. One idea was to use the bathtub as a pot for plants. You might consider this idea to be ridiculous, but that's exactly what a gardener in eastern Kansas has done. Unable to bend over because of back problems, he has collected more than 20 bathtubs for his vegetable garden. He has placed the bathtubs on concrete blocks and can still work in his garden because the bathtub gardens are now the right height.

Form New Links

In the previous example, the gardener linked a bathtub with his back problem in a new and useful way. When you are creating lists of options, it is perfectly OK to build on other ideas. If something is ridiculous, link it with another ridiculous idea. It may prove to be more useful than originally thought.

An employee with the 3M Company created a glue that wouldn't stick permanently. When he put the glue between two pieces of paper, one of the papers was easily lifted off the other. The employee was a member of his church choir and used the "useless" pieces of paper to mark the pages in his hymnal. The "useless" product is now a multimillion dollar seller for 3M. Post-it Notes® are the result of linking a failure with a need.

The number of combinations you can create is limited only by your imagination. When you use your creative-thinking skills, you can generate many more options than you have problems. In a creative climate, many of those options lead to solutions for future problems. Also, many of the options give birth to new and unexpected products and new ways of doing things.

Creative-Thinking Tools and Techniques

There are a number of creative-thinking tools and techniques for you to use in searching for new and useful connections.

Brainstorming

You've probably heard of this technique; in fact, in some organizations brainstorming has been overworked. Basically, "brainstorming" means using the guidelines for divergent thinking — postponing judgment, generating large numbers of ideas, accepting the ridiculous and forming new links. The goal in brainstorming is to write down as many options as the group can think of in a given amount time.

Brainstorming works best with a group of people who are not directly involved in the problem. You'll get different viewpoints that will generate more potential solutions. You'll need flipchart paper and someone to write down all the options that are generated. People should give their ideas in a voice loud enough for all to hear. When people hear other ideas, they use them to form new links.

A variation of brainstorming is to use Post-it Notes®. Group members write down their ideas on Post-it Notes®, read them out loud and then put the notes on a wall or board for all to see. This technique is also useful when you're alone and need to generate many options. You can collect your ideas over a period of time and put the notes in a convenient place.

Idea Writing

You can improve your thinking skills by using another variation of brainstorming, "idea writing," which also involves coming up with many ideas. Only people now write down three possible solutions and pass the paper on to someone else. If the group is not in one location, you can use idea writing for a chain letter or send it through electronic mail (E-mail).

Mind Mapping

Mind mapping is a way for you to build a word picture. Start by writing a brief statement of the problem in a circle in the center of a blank sheet of paper. Around the circle, list all the words you can think of to describe the problem. Around each of the describer words, write other words that may be connected with the describer words. When you are done, connect the words that look like they might be part of a solution.

Figure 7-1 shows part of a mind map. The problem that is mapped deals with relocating a growing business. There are a number of things to consider in this problem: good parking, green space (space for lawn and trees), close to truck facilities and staying in the same town. Good parking led to the old race track that offers truck ramps and good buildings. The desire to stay in the same town and to have green space is also met in this option. In this example, the solution is only one of many. Remember, this is a tool used to find possible solutions.

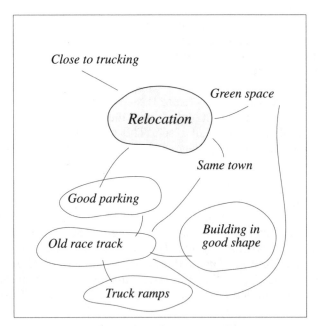

Example of Mind Mapping

Figure 7-1.

ANGLES

You can come up with large numbers of new and useful options when you look at a problem from many different "ANGLES." ANGLES stands for:

- **A**dd

- **N**ot in order

- **G**eneralize

- **L**essen

- **E**liminate

- **S**ubstitute

By changing one thing about a problem, you get a different view of the problem. For example, let's say you work for a company that makes electric golf carts. The sales of electric golf carts is decreasing because most of your customers have bought your golf carts and now they only buy replacements. Therefore, you need to find other uses for your electric golf carts.

- ***Add***. Add something to the golf cart, preferably nothing that has to do with golf. When you make the addition, you might think of another use for the electric carts. For example, add a refrigerator. It looks ridiculous, but that's OK. (Remember the third guideline for divergent thinking — "Accept the Ridiculous.") You now have an electric cart that can carry cold things around. How about an electric ice cream cart for use where there are lots of ice cream buyers — parks, ball games, picnic areas, the beach, the boardwalk? Put something else in place of the refrigerator, and you'll have other possible uses.

- ***Not in order***. Change the order of the parts on the electric golf cart. Put the steering wheel in the back. Now you have a place for the driver to stand and the passengers to sit. The electric cart can be used for moving people. It's already being done in airports; however, do not reject an idea because it's already being used. (Remember the first guideline to divergent thinking — "Postpone Judgment.") Your electric carts might be used to give people tours through museums or for rides through beautiful parks on a lazy Sunday afternoon.

- *Generalize*. Expand the problem and make it bigger. Think of the electric golf cart in broader terms, such as an electric vehicle — not just a golf cart. It could be used to move cargo instead of people. The cargo might be newspapers, mail, auto parts or baggage. Look at all the new possible customers!

- *Lessen*. Make the problem smaller. If the electric cart were smaller, you could put something on it. Maybe a sign that advertises daily lunch specials, or even advertises the cart itself. The cart is now a moving billboard.

- *Eliminate*. Take something away. Remove the motor from the golf cart and you have a seat for two that won't go anywhere. The "cart" can be used as a place to sit outside the club house.

- *Substitute*. Substitute a part or a word that describes the problem. We could replace the regular tires on the cart with large balloon tires. Now the cart can travel on sand. Lifeguards could use the carts to patrol beaches. And speaking of patrol, substitute "police" for "lifeguards" and "city parks" for "beaches." Another use is created!

ANGLES is a very powerful tool that strengthens your creative thinking skills. When you look at a problem from different ANGLES, you come up with options that no one else ever thought possible. You will be successful at creating new and useful connections.

A worksheet will help when you are working with ANGLES because it keeps a statement of the problem in front of you. It also allows you to concentrate on each of the things you want to change. When you become stumped on one word, leave it; go to another word, and return to it later. The object is to write as many changes as you can think of. The following is a completed worksheet for the golf cart problem.

ANGLES

STATEMENT OF THE PROBLEM:

What other uses are there for an electric golf cart?

Add: (Add something)

Add a refrigerator

Not in order: (Change the order)

Put the steering wheel in the back

Generalize: (Expand — make something bigger)

An electric vehicle

Lessen: (Make some part smaller)

Real tiny so it can carry a small billboard

Eliminate: (Take something away)

Take away the motor

Substitute: (Substitute a part or a word)

Balloon tires for regular tires

Following is a worksheet for you to use when you have to work on your next problem. Check to be sure that the problem has been defined correctly.

ANGLES

STATEMENT OF THE PROBLEM: *Ex: What other uses are there for an electric golf cart?*
Add: (Add something)
Not in order: (Change the order)
Generalize: (Expand — make something bigger)
Lessen: (Make some part smaller)
Eliminate: (Take something away)
Substitute: (Substitute a part or a word)

Forcing New Connections

When you need new and different solutions, use your creative thinking skills to make new connections from unrelated information. While you concentrate on the problem, look at an unrelated object. Write down the features of the object and then connect those features to your problem.

For example, you might need to cut your budget by 10 percent. As you look around the room, you see a light bulb. The features of the light bulb include: It's round, made of glass and runs on electricity. Force a connection between each of these features and your budget problem. Are the projected figures rounded up? Could your requests be more real? The glass might make you think of broken glass. Does your budget have an account for the estimated costs of vandalism? Is that account too high? The light bulb runs on electricity. Can you decrease your utility costs through an energy-saving program?

Pick any object you can see. Practice forcing new connections even when there isn't a problem. In a creative climate, the notion of forcing new connections is at work all the time. People make new connections with old products to create new products and new ways of doing things.

Visual/Audio Relaxers

The use of pictures and music as a creative thinking tool will help you through the second stage in the creative process — "Mulling It Over." Total concentration on a problem results in fewer creative solutions. The harder you try to be creative, the less creative you will be.

After you have done the groundwork for your problem, you need to take a break so you can put the information in the back of your mind. Force yourself to take a mental break by looking at pictures or listening to music.

The pictures can be nature scenes, people, food or machinery. The only condition is that the picture must not contain any words. Your mind doesn't need to see words, it just needs to look at pictures. Good sources for such pictures include magazines with good photography — *National Geographic*, *Discover* or travel brochures.

Use music that is relaxing to you. While classical and new-wave music is preferred by most, use music that makes you feel comfortable. Listen to music that has no words — just instruments playing music.

Use the visual/audio relaxers long enough to force your mind away from the problem. People with strong creative-thinking skills need from 5-15 minutes before returning to the problem. When you return to the problem, you may see a new solution immediately.

Personal Life

Select an activity in your personal life where you can use creative-thinking tools.

Career

Select an activity at work where you can use creative-thinking tools.

The Thinking Box

Select a creative-thinking tool that you will use to solve your next problem.

Select a creative-thinking tool that you will use in your personal growth plan.

Problem-Solving

Growth

Guidelines for Using Creative Tools and Techniques

Before you begin to use these tools, note the following suggestions, which will help you to be successful when using your creative-thinking skills:

- *Practice in Personal Situations*. Use new tools in personal situations before using them in business settings. During the learning process, there is always a chance that you will make mistakes, so do it privately first.

- *Document Usefulness*. When you successfully use a creative-thinking tool or technique, make a note of when and where. Some tools work best in particular situations. When similar situations come up, you'll know which tool to use, because you'll have a record of your successes.

- *Use It Soon*. A new tool can only work when you use it. If you have a new tool in your bag, you'll remember it better if you use it soon. You will have more opportunities to use the tool once you can see how it works for you.

- *Start with Low-Risk Situations*. Use your new creative-thinking tools and techniques in situations where there will be little risk if the tool doesn't work for you. Deciding where to go for lunch is a low-risk situation; picking a new Director of Planning is high-risk. Use situations where the solutions will have the smallest effect on the least number of people.

- *Use Tools and Techniques Frequently*. Use creative-thinking tools in all parts of your life. When you find a tool that works well for you, use it in your personal life and on the job. Make creative thinking a part of everything you do.

- *Find Safe Teams*. Try out some of the tools with friends before using them with your work group. Your friends will forgive you faster than your manager. For example, use creative-thinking tools to plan a picnic or vacation before you figure out how to buy more computers for your department.

Finally, you will be more creative if you "warm up" before using one of the creative-thinking tools. For example, give yourself 15 minutes and see how many uses you can find for a paper clip. If you can get a group together — seven to 10 people works best — you can find lots of ideas. This warm-up has been used with other groups, and they often find well over 50 uses for a paper clip. Many uses are ridiculous and that's fine — they followed the guidelines for creative thinking. Good luck!

Summary

You are a creative person, and you can improve your creative-thinking skills when you use tools and techniques from this chapter on your path to successful and creative solutions.

In this chapter, you learned:

- The definition of creative thinking

- How to use the creative process to help you be more creative

- Creative-thinking tools and techniques that will get your creative juices flowing

- Guidelines that will help you produce many new and useful ideas and solutions

8 ANALYTICAL THINKING

*"Two roads diverged in a wood, and I — I took the one
less traveled by, and that has made all the difference."*
— *Robert Frost*

What Is Analytical Thinking?

"Analytical thinking" is the mental activity that helps us make
correct decisions. We can use our creative-thinking skills to come up
with hundreds of solutions to our problems, but we need to use our
analytical-thinking skills to select the best solution.

As we have seen, all of our thinking is influenced by our anchors,
frames, and paradigms. When we use available analytical tools, we
get rid of the obstacles that are put in front of us by our anchors,
frames and paradigms and thereby become better able to make good
decisions and build plans that will work.

For example, when you need to make a decision about promoting
people in your department, analytical tools will give you a way to find
the most qualified person without letting friendships, for example, get
in the way of your decision.

The Role of Positive Judgment

The basic rule for analytical thinking is to force your thoughts to converge, to make them come together. This is the opposite of creative thinking where you want your thoughts to diverge, or go in different directions. When you use your analytical-thinking skills to converge your thoughts, you need to be guided by Positive Judgment, the same positive judgment discussed in Chapter 3. The guidelines for Positive Judgment are:

- Go for the Best

- Stay Organized

- Think About the New and Different

- Keep Your Eyes on the Objective

Go for the Best

When you start looking at the negatives in a solution, you'll find that all your solutions have negatives. Stay positive. Go for the best. Use your power-thinking skills to find the best possible solutions. You may end up with more than one solution. If you are the decision maker, you can then look more closely at the available solutions. If someone else is the decision maker, you can present a list of the best solutions rather than the *one* best solution. The decision maker is the one who benefits from the correct solution and suffers the consequences when a poor decision is made.

Stay Organized

When you close in on the best solution, use your strategic-thinking skills to follow an organized plan. You might be looking at 20 possible solutions to your problem. The quick way to get answers is to throw darts or roll the dice. But when you want the best answer, you need to use logical tools and techniques, and sometimes, just plain common sense.

Think About the New and Different

You spent a lot of time and energy when you used your creative-thinking skills to find new and useful ideas. And one of the reasons you used your creative thinking was to get out of a rut — always making the same decisions in the same way. You will sabotage all your work so far if you ignore the new and different. "It's always been done that way" means it's time to change. When you think of the new and different, your decisions will result in positive change.

Keep Your Eyes on the Objective

Remember the purpose for using your thinking skills. While "new and different" is important, make choices that apply to the problem. Stay in tune with your goal. If your problem is to find new customers for electric golf carts, don't go into the business of supplying security guards for parks and beaches.

Case Study: 8-1.

Robyn, the Corporate Security Chief, was looking for a good alarm system for her company's offices and received offers from all the alarm companies in town. When it was time to make a decision, some of the people in her office made comments about the alarm system — Betsey didn't like the looks of one of the sales reps, Michael didn't like the sound of another alarm and Casey knew another company that wasn't happy with a third alarm system. Robyn listened to what everyone had to say and let the people in her office sway her decision. She began to eliminate the alarm systems that people commented about and chose the one disliked by the least number of people rather than selecting the best alarm system.

Robyn based her decision on the negative feelings of the people around her. She failed to go for the best, and she failed to stay organized. As a result, she lost track of her objective — to buy a good alarm system. She relied on negative comments to make her decision.

Pitfalls to Avoid When Thinking Analytically

We can very easily fall into traps and old habits when we think analytically. When it's decision time, step away from the problem and plan your strategy. Decide what tools and techniques you are going to use to be successful. When you fail to plan, you're planning to fail. Avoid the following:

- Frame Blindness

- Lack of Frame Control

- Overconfidence

- Shooting from the Hip

- Failure to Stay on Course

Frame Blindness

"Frame blindness" means not knowing that a frame is there. You may step into a situation that is loaded with filters — yours and those of others. When you know that frames are present, you can use your thinking skills to overcome the barriers they put up. For example, you start work for a new company and your boss invites you to dinner on Saturday night. There may be a hidden frame in the company that says all good employees accept an invitation from their boss. To avoid embarrassment — and make your job easier — you need to discover the hidden frames by asking your co-workers about the "unwritten rules." Your decision on whether or not to accept the invitation can be influenced greatly by a hidden frame.

Lack of Frame Control

You may know that frames are present, but do nothing to overcome the barriers they have created. When the barriers are built by other people, you need to call "time out" and check out the reasons for the barriers. When you do, you are in control. For example, you may have given the job of putting the work schedule together to someone else. After the schedule is made out, you notice that the person who made it out always starts and leaves work one hour early in order to miss the rush-hour traffic.

No one else works a different schedule. Unless you find out why the schedule is different, you have lost frame control and could be letting someone else's frames create a barrier among your staff.

Overconfidence

When you successfully use analytical-thinking tools and techniques, you will become confident in the results; however, using tools and techniques automatically is a sign of overconfidence. Just because it worked before doesn't mean it will work again. You prevent overconfidence when you take the time to plan your work and work your plan.

Shooting from the Hip

"Shooting from the hip" means not taking aim at your objective; and it can be a sign of overconfidence. It can also show that you may not have a clear picture of the objective. Shooting from the hip is just like firing a gun blind. You hope your aim is close and that you hit the target. To avoid shooting from the hip, be sure you have a clear understanding of the objective.

Failure to Stay on Course

To use your thinking skills successfully, you need to stay on course. When bombarded with distractions from many sources, it is difficult to stay on track. Create a detailed plan and avoid distractions — this will keep you headed in the right direction.

Tools and Techniques for Analytical Thinking

To help you stay organized in your search for the best answers, you can use the following tools and techniques, which will help you *go for the best, stay organized, think about the new and different* and *keep your eyes on the objective.*

The Priority Grid

When you have a number of options that you want to compare, you can use the Priority Grid. It helps you build an anchor so that you can use your analytical thinking skills effectively. The grid is used to rank options according to their importance. The options must be stated in the same form. For example, one option might read: "Spend more money on advertising." If a second option reads, "Save money on maintenance," the two options are not expressed in the same form. One is positive and the other is written as a negative. The second option needs to say, "Spend less money on maintenance." The options must also be written concisely. Instead of "spend money," use "spend $110,000," or whatever is appropriate.

1. Write the options to be weighed in the column labeled "Options." You are not limited to five options. You may have more or fewer.

2. Work down the first row under the column labeled "Choices," and decide which is more important, Option A or Option B. Write the letter of your choice in the top left box.

3. Decide which level of importance to give to your choice, and write the number from the scale at the bottom of the Priority Grid.

4. Continue to go down the first row on the left, then down Row B, and so on, until you have filled in all the boxes.

5. When you are finished, find all the boxes marked "A" and total the scores. Write the total on the line under the column labeled "Sum of Scores." Do the same for all the other options.

You can also use the Priority Grid to get agreement within a group. Now each group member completes a Priority Grid and all the "Sum of Scores" are put on one group Priority Grid to come up with a "Group Sum of Scores."

The Priority Grid

SUM OF SCORES	OPTIONS	CHOICES

SUM OF
SCORES

OPTIONS

CHOICES

_____ A. _____ A.

_____ B. _____ B.

_____ C. _____ C.

_____ D. _____ D.

_____ E. _____

Scale:
1 = More Important
2 = A Little More Important
3 = A Lot More Important

My No. 1 Option is _____ .
My No. 2 Option is _____ .
My No. 3 Option is _____ .
My No. 4 Option is _____ .
My No. 5 Option is _____ .

Following is an example of how the Priority Grid works. In this case the Priority Grid is used to help prioritize tasks that need to be done tomorrow. When the Priority Grid is completed, you can see how the tasks are listed in order of importance.

Make a Priority Grid for yourself and watch how it keeps you organized and on track. If something comes up tomorrow that you didn't expect, just make it fit into your Priority Grid and reorganize.

The Priority Grid

SUM OF SCORES	OPTIONS	CHOICES				
7	A. *Ship package by Air Express*	A.				
4	B. *Call Human Resources*	B2	B.			
0	C. *Finish expense report*	A3	B2	C.		
8	D. *Meet with staff*	A1	D3	D3	D.	
6	E. *Schedule vacations*	A3	E3	D2	E3	

Scale:
1 = More Important
2 = A Little More Important
3 = A Lot More Important

My No. 1 Option is	*Meet with the staff.*
My No. 2 Option is	*Ship the package by Air Express.*
My No. 3 Option is	*Schedule vacations.*
My No. 4 Option is	*Call Human Resources.*
My No. 5 Option is	*Finish the expense report.*

The Ps 'n Qs Tool

The Ps 'n Qs tool looks at the **P**ositives, **N**egatives and **Q**uirks in an idea or solution. It gives you a way to stay organized when you need to look deeper into an idea or solution.

The Ps 'n Qs tool gets you started by letting you use your power-thinking skills to look first at all the positive features — the strong points — of a solution. You may have to stretch your mind and use your creative-thinking skills to come up with all the positive features, but this tool lets you look at solutions that are new and different.

Not every solution is going to be 100 percent perfect, however, so there may also be some negative features that you need to think about. List the negative features in the form of questions. When you can answer the question, you may be able to turn a negative into a positive. For example, you see a negative feature that tells you that the solution will cost too much. Change your writing to read, "How can I afford to pay for this?" If you can answer the question, the feature is no longer a negative.

Quirks are twists, oddities or variations. When you look at the quirks, you force yourself to look for new and different solutions. You are intentionally asking yourself the question, "What is there that makes this solution different from others?" This step will help you stay out of that "same-decision-every-time" rut.

Deciding on a restaurant for dinner is a nice, safe place to use the Ps 'n Qs tool the first time. You will probably find yourself enjoying a new dining experience!

The Ps 'n Qs Tool

POSITIVE:
What are the strong points and positive features of this option?

NEGATIVES:
What are the negative features of this option? (Remember to word your responses in the form of a question.)

QUIRKS:
What makes this option different from other options? What are the variations or oddities?

The Options/Criteria Worksheet

When you have a number of options that you need to match with a number of criteria, you'll find the Options/Criteria Worksheet very helpful on the way to making correct decisions. The worksheet allows you to select the standards against which to compare your options.

If you are unsure of what criteria to use, apply your creative-thinking skills to find appropriate criteria. Criteria can come from a number of places and may apply to only one situation. Criteria are used to rate and select the best options so that you can be successful in your decision-making.

After you have selected your options, write them in the first column of your worksheet. Then write the criteria in the blank spaces across the top. You can use as many or as few columns as you need. Be sure, however, that the criteria are written in the same form. "Increased productivity" is not in the same form as "a decrease in customer complaints." You need to change the negative statement into a positive, such as "increased customer satisfaction."

Complete the worksheet by going down each column and, using the Rating Scale, rate all options against one criterion at a time. Complete the criteria for all options before moving to the next column. Otherwise, if you have a favorite option, it will get a higher score if you go across the worksheet. By going down the columns, you will get more honest ratings.

You can use any rating scale that works for you. One has been provided, but you may already have one with which you are familiar. After filling in all the boxes, total the scores for each option. You are using a tool to keep you organized and help you make correct decisions.

THE OPTIONS/CRITERIA WORKSHEET

OPTIONS	CRITERIA						Totals
1.							
2.							
3.							
4.							
5.							
6.							

RATING SCALE: 1 = POOR   4 = VERY GOOD
2 = OK   5 = OUTSTANDING
3 = GOOD

Following is an example of how to use the Options/Criteria Worksheet. Suppose you need to pick one of the people on your staff to serve as your assistant. The qualities you are looking for in your assistant are "loyal, capable, never late, likable and creative." Notice that all the qualities are stated in a positive way, except "never late." You need to change it to a positive trait, such as "on time." Enter the employees' names under the Options column and put the qualities under the Criteria column. Then rate the employees for loyalty before rating how capable they are.

THE OPTIONS/CRITERIA WORKSHEET

OPTIONS		CRITERIA					Totals
		Loyal	Capable	On Time	Likable	Creative	
1.	Wayne	5	4	3	5	5	22
2.	Florence	4	3	2	5	2	16
3.	Ryan	2	2	4	3	1	12
4.	Rick	3	4	5	1	2	15
5.	Louise	1	5	4	5	3	18
6.	Sally	3	3	2	3	2	13

RATING SCALE: 1 = POOR   4 = VERY GOOD
2 = OK   5 = OUTSTANDING
3 = GOOD

As you can see from this example, everyone received at least a 5 rating for one of the criteria. When you rate each individual against one criterion at a time, you get a better overall picture of the person you want as your assistant.

Selecting the Right Tool

Sometimes the hardest job is finding the right tool. The following chart will help. Determine which statement in the first column matches your need, then select the right tool from the second column.

??? What Tool to Use When ???	
When you have . . .	**Use . . .**
To prioritize your options	the Priority Grid
Many options that need to meet certain criteria	the Options/Criteria Worksheet
One or a few options	the Ps 'n Qs Tool

Personal Life

Select activities in your personal life where you can use each of the analytical-thinking tools.

Career

Select activities at work where you can use each of the analytical-thinking tools.

The Thinking Box

Select a problem that you have solved and rehearse how to use each of the analytical-thinking tools.

Select one of the analytical-thinking tools to make a decision about your personal or professional growth.

Problem-Solving

Growth

Summary

In this chapter on analytical thinking, you learned:

- When to use analytical thinking

- The importance of Positive Judgment when you need to converge your thoughts

- Pitfalls to avoid when thinking analytically

- Analytical-thinking tools and techniques

  - The Priority Grid

  - The Ps 'n Qs tool

  - The Options/Criteria Worksheet

9 MORE THAN THINKING ABOUT THINKING

"You know you are both good and ready when you can beat an opponent on pure, business-like terms without getting hot and bothered about it."

— *Jim Valvano*

The Rethinking Model brings together the four types of thinking skills you need to be successful in your personal life and your career — Strategic Thinking, Power Thinking, Creative Thinking and Analytical Thinking. Each is not separate from the others, but rather part of the whole model. Most people are familiar with each of the types, but the key to success is to use all types of thinking at the same time. When you use the Rethinking Model, you will have the answers you need to *Who, What, When, Where, Why* and *How*. You will make the "right" decisions, and the "right" decisions will make you successful!

When you finish reading ***The Power of Innovative Thinking*** and put it on your bookshelf, your thinking skills will not magically improve — unless **YOU** want them to! You are in control of the way you think.

Powerful-thinking skills put you in control of situations instead of allowing situations to control you. Take the time to ***THINK***, and after reading this book, take the time to ***THINK ABOUT THINKING***. You will stay in control.

When you are in control, you no longer handle problems in a reactive way — a crisis every time. Instead, you can concentrate on being **PROACTIVE** — ready for any situation. When you are proactive, you know that your solutions will lead to correct decisions. Your results will be positive and, therefore, *YOU* will be *POSITIVE*.

Once you accept the power of positive thinking, you can achieve any goal you set for yourself. You will *CONTINUE TO LEARN*. And whether you continue to learn in a formal setting or each and every day in an informal way, you'll discover that knowledge can be a powerful tool. If you want to be successful at your job and in your personal life, you must continually seek to improve your thinking skills.

You have the power of choice, and the choice is yours!

- **THINK**

- **THINK ABOUT THINKING**

- **BE PROACTIVE**

- **CHOOSE TO BE POSITIVE**

- **CONTINUE TO LEARN**

When you use your thinking skills to get to your goals, you will be successful. "Success" is not "reaching a goal" — it is THE PATHWAY TO THE GOAL. And the pathway to the goal gets easier, not by thinking harder but by thinking smarter!

May your successes be a result of thinking smarter.

Index

Notes

Buy any 3, get 1 FREE!

Get a 60-Minute Training Series™ Handbook FREE ($14.95 value)* when you buy any three. See back of order form for full selection of titles.

These are helpful how-to books for you, your employees and co-workers. Add to your library. Use for new-employee training, brown-bag seminars, promotion gifts and more. Choose from many popular titles on a variety of lifestyle, communication, productivity and leadership topics. Exclusively from National Press Publications.

DESKTOP HANDBOOK ORDER FORM

Ordering is easy:

1. Complete both sides of this Order Form, detach, and mail, fax or phone your order to:

    Mail: National Press Publications
    P.O. Box 419107
    Kansas City, MO 64141-6107

    Fax: 1-913-432-0824
    Phone: 1-800-258-7248
    Internet: www.natsem.com

2. Please print:

Name_____ Position/Title _____

Company/Organization_____

Address_____City _____

State/Province_____ZIP/Postal Code _____

Telephone (____)_____ Fax (____) _____

Your e-mail: _____

3. Easy payment:

❑ Enclosed is my check or money order for $_____ (total from back).
Please make payable to National Press Publications.

Please charge to:
❑ MasterCard   ❑ VISA   ❑ American Express

Credit Card No. _____ Exp. Date_____

Signature_____

● ●
MORE WAYS TO SAVE:
SAVE 33%!!! BUY 20-50 COPIES of any title ... pay just $9.95 each ($11.25 Canadian).

SAVE 40%!!! BUY 51 COPIES OR MORE of any title ... pay just $8.95 each ($10.25 Canadian).

* $20.00 in Canada

Buy 3, get 1 FREE!
60-MINUTE TRAINING SERIES™ HANDBOOKS

TITLE	RETAIL PRICE	QTY	TOTAL
8 Steps for Highly Effective Negotiations #424	$14.95		
Assertiveness #4422	$14.95		
Balancing Career and Family #4152	$14.95		
Common Ground #4122	$14.95		
Delegate for Results #4592	$14.95		
The Essentials of Business Writing #4310	$14.95		
Everyday Parenting Solutions #4862	$14.95		
Exceptional Customer Service #4882	$14.95		
Fear & Anger: Slay the Dragons … #4302	$14.95		
Fundamentals of Planning #4301	$14.95		
Getting Things Done #4112	$14.95		
How to Coach an Effective Team #4308	$14.95		
How to De-Junk Your Life #4306	$14.95		
How to Handle Conflict and Confrontation #4952	$14.95		
How to Manage Your Boss #493	$14.95		
How to Supervise People #4102	$14.95		
How to Work With People #4032	$14.95		
Inspire & Motivate: Performance Reviews #4232	$14.95		
Listen Up: Hear What's Really Being Said #4172	$14.95		
Motivation and Goal-Setting #4962	$14.95		
A New Attitude #4432	$14.95		
The New Dynamic Comm. Skills for Women #4309	$14.95		
The Polished Professional #4262	$14.95		
The Power of Innovative Thinking #428	$14.95		
The Power of Self-Managed Teams #4222	$14.95		
Powerful Communication Skills #4132	$14.95		
Present With Confidence #4612	$14.95		
The Secret to Developing Peak Performers #4692	$14.95		
Self-Esteem: The Power to Be Your Best #4642	$14.95		
Shortcuts to Organized Files & Records #4307	$14.95		
The Stress Management Handbook #4842	$14.95		
Supreme Teams: How to Make Teams Work #4303	$14.95		
Thriving on Change #4212	$14.95		
Women and Leadership #4632	$14.95		

Sales Tax All purchases subject to state and local sales tax. Questions? Call **1-800-258-7248**	Subtotal	$
	Add 7% Sales Tax (*Or add appropriate state and local tax*)	$
	Shipping and Handling (*$3 one item; 50¢ each additional item*)	$
	TOTAL	$

08/01